FROM MINIMUM WAG

THE POWER WITHIN YOU

LEARN TO CREATE A HAPPY, HEALTHY, PROFITABLE LIFE

CHRIS CARLEY

Clovercroft Publishing

The Power within You

© 2019 by Chris Carley

Published by Clovercroft Publishing, Franklin, Tennessee

Cover Design by Nelly Sanchez

Interior Design by Symbiosys Technologies

Edited by Christy Callahan

Printed in the United States of America

978-1-948484-82-4

ACKNOWLEDGEMENTS

Thanks to my little sister Becky and Mom for taking care of me when life got rough, instilling in me the Power of God and always cheering me on.

And thanks to the other men in my life who taught me so much: Jim Rohn, Donald Trump and my dear Grandfathers Floyd Carley SR. and Dean Holgate who gave me my values and strong work ethics. Thank you to my fifth and sixth grade teachers at Chinook Elementary in Auburn, WA; Mr. Kurt Aust and Mr. Rollins for loving all my short stories, encouraging me to keep writing and believing in me. A big thanks to Don Dedo for introducing me to my book team at OnFire Books.

Last but never, ever least, thank you Bob Anderson for motivating me to write my lead book and first package system that helped so many make 6 figure incomes in their first year of utilizing your and Joe Flaherty's ideas, allowing me to make my first million so quickly and over 20 million to date. You are truly one in a million.

CONTENTS

INTRODUCTION

What's Your Definition of Success?

Success, money, and happiness don't come just to special, talented, or lucky people. Within each of us lie the answers and direction we need to create unlimited abundance, and you can choose a path to realize your dreams that is joyful and easy. You do that by plugging into the universal power and intelligence available to all of us.

My transition from factory worker to network marketer didn't happen overnight. In fact, I was reluctant at first. I didn't want to be scammed or have someone take advantage of me. Even when I got going, it still wasn't all roses. There was a constant battle with my outer reality and the inner reality I was working to reshape.

The Difficulty of Evolving

Write this down: "For things to change, I have to change. For things to get better, I have to get better. My spouse doesn't need to change, nor do my family, job, or my circumstance need to change. For things to change for me, I have to change."

Jim Rohn gave these words to all of us attending his speech. He instructed us to put those words up somewhere where we could see them, and read them out loud three times a day for ninety days, consecutively. He cautioned us that only 1 in 40,000 would follow through.

> **For things to change, you have to change. For things to get better, you have to get better.For things to improve, you have to improve. When you grow, everything in your life grows with you.**
>
> **JIM ROHN**

"Some of you will follow through for thirty days, then miss a day or forget to do it three times a day, and have to start over again." He smiled and waved his arm around the whole stadium.

"Some of you will make it to sixty days." He paused dramatically, challenging each one of us as his smile got even bigger.

"Some of you will make it almost to ninety days." His voice grew pained as it trailed off, and then he delivered the next word with power: "*One*...one of you will make it all one hundred twenty days, and that person will be up here onstage with me, earning millions."

Forty thousand people started clapping, but he motioned with his hands to stop, and we waited, sitting forward, anxious for his next instruction.

"Tape up your goals," he continued. "Somewhere in your home where you will see it the most and read it out loud three times a day for one hundred twenty days, consecutively."

"Your first step in reaching success is to know what you want and to remind your subconscious everyday what it is. Do not worry about the 'how.' Write down what it is you want!"

My teeth began to chatter as electricity flew through me. His words activated knowledge hidden in my DNA. High school teachers had taught us that the earth generates its own magnetic field, but they never went into how it all worked. How did all the planets know to line up in just the exact right positions? What force, or Intelligence, keeps the Universe in perfect order? Religions from around the world call it by different names, but it's still the same. There is a guiding intelligence we can all tap into.

"I want to knooooow," he shouted into his microphone, "who's it going to be?!"

Forty-thousand people from 47 different countries exploded out of their chairs, raising their hands, shouting, "Me, it's going to be me!"

Still hunched over my notebook, a stack of sticky notes in front of me, I furiously wrote my goals down on each small square without looking up. I didn't realize I was the only one in the stadium still seated.

If one sticky note put up for that amount of time would make me a millionaire, how much would hundreds of little notes stuck up everywhere make me?

$10,000/month checks
Safari in Africa
Porsche
Beach House in California on the water
Travel the world helping others
Have great Friends
Cruise the world
Help family buy homes
Charity

Jim Rohn reinforced what we all know. Our thoughts—what we focus on, dream about, talk about—open us to ideas that lead us to opportunities. Jim was reigniting something inside me, and I felt hope—a dangerous feeling if you don't have a plan, but invigorating if you've got a map showing you a way to reach your goals.

What We All Know

Life is a combination of hard work and intentionality, and I hope through reading my story and the lessons I have learned about marketing, myself, and my business, you will experience the same success I did. If you follow the basic marketing rules outlined throughout this book, combined with the "Laws of Attraction," nothing can stop you.

As you travel on your own journey, you'll pick up your own lessons along the way. Everything we do comes from the foundation of knowledge and experience. As you read through the pages of this book, I hope you can gain wisdom to apply in your own life.

CHAPTER 1

Adventures of Owning Your Own Business

A lot of people look at the success I've had in the network marketing industry and think it came from nowhere. For years I struggled unsuccessfully in business endeavors that didn't work, because I wasn't tapped into the "Universal Intelligence" that directs us all, if we let it. All my life, everyone I knew was on the brink of financial ruin, working hard, long hours for big corporations that would lay our breadwinners off, or cause hardship through months of striking without pay. Fear and uncertainty were with us at all times.

Direct Sales and The Man

When I was younger, my parents moved us out on a farm that wasn't anything fancy, but it was a far cry from the city life I knew. It was also the first place I began to exercise my entrepreneurial creativity.

At least two hours, twice a week, plus anytime I was in trouble and sentenced to my room for doing something I wasn't supposed to, I dreamed of ways to make money so my father wouldn't have to work so hard and could be with us more often. One of those weeks I took all of my savings, from mowing the lawn to picking berries during the summer, to invest in one little expensive vial of pure cinnamon oil. I took the oil and soaked toothpicks it, making cinnamon toothpicks, which was all the craze. I ended up selling them at school for a penny a piece.

I did so well that 20 to 30 kids were sucking on them at recess. Thirty cents may not be a big deal now, but it was the world to me, and I could feel I was on to something. That same day some of the teachers took notice. They began to worry that someone might fall and choke on one. I'm not sure who it was, but one my classmates ratted me out to my teacher, and I promptly found myself sitting in the principal's office.

In my family, being sent to the principal's office meant double punishment. My legs were shaking and my face was bright red as I stumbled into his office. I knew that the next thing that was going to happen was a call to my parents, and I hated the thought of disappointing them. That was the first day I learned about the challenges of being a creative self-starter. When you think differently, not everyone is going to support you. I was an entrepreneur at heart, but it didn't mean there weren't going to be obstacles in the way.

The principal sat me down, paused, and looked at me for a moment. Then he spoke. "Christine, I am proud of your business skills, but the teachers are worried the kids will get hurt with the toothpicks. Would you please stop selling them at school."

Relief spread across my chest. I nodded yes and quickly got out of there. I still needed to figure out how to make money though. Throughout my life I embarked on this quest to make things happen. It all stemmed from my early child hood experiences watching my parents manage their own life, family, and finances.

Walnuts Taught Me Everything

The next project was buying a calf for 4-H. Attending the meetings at my friends' homes was embarrassing. They all had top-bred, prize-winning animals, and I had nothing. My parents told me I could join, but they weren't buying me any kind of animal until I proved that I was committed to the 4-H cause.

So every month I would attend the 4-H meetings mortified. I would stand there, pretending I had a calf. As the others were shown how to clean the hooves and ears of their calves, I would listen intently and go through the motions on my pretend calf. While they were being taught the general care of their steers and heifers, I could see some of the kids making fun of me. A few even turned the garden hose on me to irritate me. Nevertheless, I was determined.

The chance to redeem myself came in the form of nuts, bags and bags of walnuts. 4-H was having a fund-raising drive to benefit the local fair. All of the members had to sell bags of walnuts, even the ones with calves. I was born competitive, and although I wasn't excited about selling walnuts, I pictured myself selling the most.

I wanted to win the contest, so I began by asking my mom if she needed any walnuts for her brownies or cookies. Half expecting her to say no, I told her what the walnuts' price per pound was. I had never seen my mom so enthusiastic. On the spot she bought all of my bags of walnuts. Then she asked me if I could get more. I grinned. In that moment I felt like I had a chance at winning.

The next day she drove me back to the farm of our 4-H leader. The woman looked amazed that I had sold everything and already needed more. Handing her the cash, I asked for double the amount this time. Her words shook my confidence. "Are you sure? You're awful little to be handling so many walnuts."

My face burned bright red, and I just stood there staring at her, saying nothing.

"How 'bout we give you just a couple pounds again and see how you do."

After standing there, looking at the ground, I just nodded, took what she gave me, and headed back to the car.

Mom saw the look on my face, the small bag of walnuts, and said, "You go back in there and tell her you need more."

"I did. She wouldn't give them to me. She said I was too little."

"Come on." Mom, in her bathrobe and slippers, marched across the wet grass toward the barn. I ran behind. I was so happy to have my mom sticking up for me.

The 4-H leader's farm was nothing like ours. Everything shone new in the morning sun. Her fence was perfect and bright white, which matched the barn's trim, and $10,000 prize bulls and award-winning Black Angus cattle munched on expensive hay. The bulls and cattle lazily turned their heads to look at us with curious eyes.

My mom approached the 4-H leader, who was now brushing down a nervous pure-blood race horse, and said, "Excuse me. I just took the time to drive my daughter over here so she could get more walnuts to sell."

Shocked by my mom's irritation, the 4-H leader stopped brushing the horse and turned to my mom. Before she could say anything, Mom said, "You don't know my daughter, but I do, and she would like thirty more pounds of walnuts please."

"Sure." The lady smiled. "There's no bringing them back, you know."

Finally, my anger at her snide remarked allowed me to stick up for myself. "Have any of the other kids sold all their walnuts you gave us last night?" I asked.

"Well, no, but I'm sure..." Seeing the determination in me, she handed over the 30 pounds of walnuts to me. I carried them all to the car, staggering under the weight.

"She can't even lift them!" The woman pointed out to my mom.

Ignoring the woman, Mom marched back to the car, head down, dodging manure land mines. "You have to understand what you have here. Good walnuts are hard to come by, and every mother or wife is baking cookies, pies, brownies—all kinds of things—this summer."

Eager, I opened the glove compartment, got some paper out, and found an old pen and started to add to Mom's list of all the things walnuts could be used for: banana bread, fudge, salads, ice cream, cereal, carrot cake. Then I made a list of everyone I knew who might want to buy walnuts from me. Living out of town on a farm with only a few neighbors was not going to slow me down.

I began writing. Grandma cooked a lot, Grandma's friends cooked stuff with walnuts, all the ladies at church, a new neighbor with four kids had just moved in...

"You know, I could drop you off in different neighborhoods across town and you could go door-to-door."

"Okay, after I get everyone out here where there are no grocery stores," I said.

Mom smiled.

* * *

As soon as we got home, I tied a bag of walnuts to my bike's handlebars and on the back fender. I also picked up one in my arms and planned to ride one-handed, but decided against that after I crashed. Going to the only three neighbors in our area, I had a warm reception. After my carefully planned pitch about all the things they could use walnuts for, each woman smiled and laughed. In fact, they all wanted a bag.

Then I upsold them (I didn't know what that was back then), making sure to let them know that I was the youngest and smallest kid in 4-H who had already sold the most walnuts, capping it off by saying, "And I'm going to win first prize." That made the women buy another bag, and they didn't even care when I told them. I didn't even know what the first prize was.

Then I asked if they knew anyone at their church, work, or any family members that might want walnuts. Instinctively I had asked for referrals. They were glad to give me phone numbers of people they knew would want them.

Both of my grandmas bought five bags each. My maternal grandmother gave me the telephone numbers of her friends. As a kid, I hated calling or even talking to someone I didn't know on the telephone—but I forced myself to dial the numbers. Even though I stuttered when I made my pitch, I sold all four of Grandma's friends.

The next day, when we showed back up at the 4-H leader's house, she didn't say a word as I handed her the money and asked for double the amount of bags again. The contest only lasted until the end of summer, and Mom had Dad take some bags to work, and I wrote up a little paper on all the things walnuts could be used for him to show his co-workers.

Mom drove me to Seattle to deliver Grandma Carley's walnuts. Nan had a list of her friends that lived nearby and Grandpa heard that dad had sold five bags, so he bought seven bags from me to sell at work the next day. Gramps was really helpful too.

One day, when I went with Mom to get groceries, I saw some of the older kids who had made fun of me for not having a calf trying to sell their walnuts outside the store. They looked miserable. They obviously had been there for a while, because their clothes were sweaty and their faces sunburned, and it looked like none of them had sold a thing.

Lessons Learned and Shared

Don't let anyone steal your dreams. Get your family and loved ones to believe in you by showing determination. That 4-H lady didn't believe in me, but instead of letting that stop me, I let it make me more passionate about succeeding.

Know your product. Sell something that is consumable and that you are excited about.

You will have difficulties, but when you understand that every successful salesperson and company had those same obstacles and overcame them, then you can too.

To get more, you need to become more. The only way to do that is to study and learn your craft. Before you get on the phone to anyone, spend at least 15 minutes on *how* to tap into the Universal Intelligence. Get the book *The Magic of Believing* by Claude Bristol and *TNT: Tt Rocks the Earth*. Those words will change your entire day and allow you to attract easily and effortlessly.

CHAPTER 2

Picture This

Imagine a woman, dead broke with over $30,000 in debt. A woman in a horrible, unsatisfying marriage, a woman whose health was so bad that she couldn't get out of bed some days. That was me. I was a long way from the little girl who excitedly sold walnuts for 4-H that one summer. I don't say this for you to have sympathy or to feel bad for me. In fact, I want you to celebrate with me and see that if I could make that first step toward changing my circumstances, so can you.

At that time in my life, all of my friends and family were steering clear of me. I had lost my hostile work environment case against Boeing and owed my attorneys over $30,000. Earlier business opportunities I had introduced to my family and friends had failed miserably. I felt it was because of my lack of experience, education, and my eroding self esteem. I felt toxic, and for the first time in my life, not only was I out of shape, but I was also fat. I wanted to and needed to make a change, but I didn't know how to start.

As I began praying and asking for guidance, right away I started remembering from my grade school years a teacher who had told us about how words affect us. I realized I had been telling myself the wrong story.

The Mind-Body Connection

In the movie *Out of Africa*, Robert Redford tells Meryl Streep that when men from African tribes were put into captivity, they died because they couldn't understand that one day they would be released. I think people who commit suicide must feel that way too. Books on depression reveal that suicidal thoughts are often contemplated by persons experiencing debilitating waves of despair when they don't think the future will be any different. Lying on the couch, vegetating in front of the television—hour after hour after hour for months—reliving my failures, losses, and unfair circumstances, I found myself engulfed by depression so heavily, so painfully that I couldn't bear it anymore.

So I'd go to a doctor and spend an hour talking about my problems and re-experiencing the awful feelings of hopelessness, worrying out loud that each day for the rest of my life would be the same, the misery never going away. The thought that I would always be like that, I'd never laugh again, or feel good or want to do anything, or be passionate about something ever in my life, left me feeling even worse. I'd come out of the psychiatrist's office shaking, crying, sometimes even throwing up.

The more the doctor had me talk about bad experiences, the more I noticed the world's hardships. *What is the reason any of us are even here? What is my purpose? What am I supposed to be doing here? If there really is a reason for everything that happens, what is it?!*

Sick of myself, tired of the couch, I rolled to my knees and prayed for understanding. Then I waited, and when nothing happened, no ideas or booming voice from the heavens answered, I flopped on the floor defeated, tears rolling out of the corners of swollen red eyes. *How can I have any tears left? What happened to that girl who hit home runs so easily?*

Since the verdict, I had done nothing but cram food down my throat, and I was easily 40 pounds overweight, disgustingly pushing the scales at 170 pounds. Everything I read about depression said exercise and changing negative thoughts to positive would snap the afflicted back to "normal."

Dragging myself off the tear-stained rug, I searched through the month-long scattered clothes, trying to find something warm to wear so I wouldn't freeze, my bed calling me to come back. I tried desperately to think of anything good in my life. Nothing. Then a glimmer of some forgotten fragment buried deep in my brain started to surface, and I remembered segments of a book I had been reading during my lunches at Boeing.

Change Your Thoughts

As I focused, a thought grew, bringing to mind, *You are what you think about.* This memory brought forth tiny old feelings of confidence and energy I possessed back before I lost my job at Boeing, and I saw my old self bent over a book, scribbling furiously on my notepad, underlining passages, unaware of anything or anyone, smiling whenever I read something that really struck home.

The book was very old, written in 1930, but I couldn't remember the name. If I could relive every detail of bad times, couldn't I do the same with the times I'd felt good? Forgetting present time, I felt the coldness of the shop, the isolating breaks that had allowed me to study human psych for years, then zoomed in on the title, but could only "see" the author's name: Claude Bristol.

Instantly I recalled the title, *The Magic of Believing.* Eerily the book's words flooded not only my intellect, but my body. The entire premise of the old book taught that anyone could think their way into better circumstances thus changing their lives. Zig Ziglar had written an introduction telling the reader: "This little book... changed my life from 'poverty, despair and defeat into happiness and richness beyond imagination.'"

Running to my boxes of books, I found it on the top, and opening it, again the words hit me in the face. "For those of you who seek to learn and make progress, I gently lay this message in your laps. I do so without the slightest fear but that it will turn your world entirely upside down—bringing you health, wealth, success and happiness, provided you understand and accept it."

Reading the words, I remembered why I had been selected out of thousands of smarter people trying out for *Wheel of Fortune*! For months, I had concentrated on seeing myself winning on the show. I wasn't worried about not making the cut, because I had pictured myself spinning the wheel and winning!

"This power can be proved by the teachings of the Bible, certain well-established laws of physics and, last but not least, just plain common sense."

How could I have forgotten this?

Because for the last two years ALL your thoughts have been focused on the horrible atrocities that surrounded you daily at work and then again in court. I answered myself, then, *Keep reading* came into my head, and I continued reading. "Nothing in this world is so powerful as an idea whose time has come" (Victor Hugo.)

Wow! That had been the answer to the puzzle on *Wheel of Fortune* that I had won so much money from! Goosebumps exploded on my arm, the hair standing straight up.

"The time has come for the greatest idea in the world to take possession of your consciousness. It is a simple idea, but when you open up your mind and let it in, you'll never be the same again."

This is why I had been fired from a job that almost killed me. There was a better place for me than that factory job. I hadn't forgotten any of it; it had always been there in my brain cells, but had temporarily disappeared from lack of use.

Serving My Time at Boeing

My brain, now fired and working fast, flashed me back to the memory of reading these same books during lunch. A new co-worker about my mother's age that I was training—we will call her "Janet"—had just left the lunch group of hateful girls and had walked back to our area. Lighting a cigarette, then blowing smoke at me, knowing I was deathly allergic to it, she looked at book, laughed, and shook her perfectly coiffed, bleached-blonde, mother-beehive-styled head.

"What?" I challenged.

Chuckle, chuckle, chuckle, roll of the eyes, shake of the head. "Chris, you're *not* special."

Startled, her mean words hit me. "Did you really just say that?" I choked.

Flicking her cigarette ashes at me, she pointed to my book. "Every day I see you reading those books thinking that they'll help you get out of here, but you won't. You're just like all of us, and thirty years from now you'll still be here."

I opened another book I'd studied, Charles Haanel's *Master Key System*. "Janet, this book was written in the forties, and the same principle is used in every book on success, including the Bible. It's a scientific fact that our bodies are made up of atoms, and our thoughts affect—"

Pushing the book away, she got into my face, her yellow teeth and bad smoke breath forcing me to recoil. "Listen to me, " she croaked. "*You're nobody special.* It's a joke that you think you'll be the 'one' that makes it out of here."

"Come on, Janet! There are millions of people who are thriving, who have second and third homes. All we have to do is find out what they know and do it."

Still shaking her head, she ignored me, pushing her cart down to where the gaggle of negative women still congregated, replaying our conversation to them, peals of shrill laughter heard all over the shop.

Going in the opposite direction to work in a connecting building, I felt myself slowing down and my shoulders sinking. There wasn't anyone in my life I could even talk to about these books. I felt churning in my stomach and a knot tightening with good old FEAR. Would I really be here the next 30 years? My father had and his father before him.

As anxiety and trepidation flooded through me, my body began to change chemically. My heart rate dropped, my facial muscles slackened, and my movement became clumsy. The clock ticked more slowly, but the last paragraph I was reading before Janet rudely slapped the book out of my hands hit me, so I ducked into the bathroom to read it again.

FACT: We all have over a trillion cells in our bodies with each cell having its own consciousness. When the brain is given a thought from our mind, the

cerebrospinal system of nerves puts conscious communication with every part of our body based on whatever thought we are thinking. The system of nerves responds to every sensation: taste, sound, pain, light, heat, cold. Whatever thoughts we send to the cerebro-spinal nervous system determines what our body feels and reacts.

This made sense to me. If I think of biting into a peeled lemon, really chomping on it, instantly my mouth starts to water. My face scrunches up, I have to swallow. This proved that thoughts don't have to be real for our bodies to react. My body automatically responds to the thought! If I think sad and depressing thoughts, I feel bad, and my body responds. If I think about good stuff...

Trying to Squash That Negative Inner Voice

I remember so clearly at the time the two voices that were waging an internal war within me. I started to argue with myself.

But there isn't any good in my life now. I've got a job I hate. My life is awful.

You've got two arms and two legs. You are in shape. Something, some energy answered.

I have a loveless, lousy marriage, and working midnight to seven is making me sick.

You've done it before—been successful in starting your own trucking business.

But...I lost everything!

You had no control over the oilfield crashing. You've learned from it! You are still young!

Oh God, what am I going to do to get out of here?

Flipping through the pages, I got the answer and read:

"You do not need to know the HOW, you need only visualize, dwell upon the outcome wanted."

But it hurts to think about what I don't have.

Just do it.

I could clomp through work, focusing on what Janet had said and get upset, or I could follow through with what every bestseller taught and replace my negative fears.

Okay, where do I start? I know what I don't want. What do I want? I want to have a job where I change people's lives and make a lot of money. I want to be a millionaire, living in Malibu, California, on the beach, in the sun.

I left the bathroom feeling better.

I began to picture in detail a big white wide-open beachfront home, with the ocean as my front yard. It didn't work. Doubts and fear and the sensation of grief swallowed me whole, and I ducked into an empty office, sobbing, shoulders shaking, hopelessness weighing me down until I was sitting on the cold, filthy cement floor.

"It" wasn't working. There is no way my dreams were going to happen here, and my body wasn't fooled by the thought. In fact, it seemed mad. I understood I wasn't to worry about the "how" part of it but keep picturing what I want and then listen if I get an idea or inspiration to do something. But from the dungeon I'm trapped in here to a place in Malibu? Maybe I should focus on something smaller, like a better job or seeing myself living in a sunshine-filled state.

As I did my menial job, I started to picture myself happy and walking along a beach. Three hours later when the alarm for our last ten-minute break sounded, I grabbed my book and opened it. I sat frozen. On almost every page, something awful and obscene had been written in thick black permanent ink. Those awful girls watched from a distance, laughing. This time I felt sorry for them. They would be here for the next 30 years. I would not.

Ignoring them, I opened the book and read: "This idea will shake you to the foundations of your being. It will destroy old false concepts and replace them with new ones. It will eventually remove fear and worry from your life. It will release you from chronic nervous tensions, chase the butterflies out of your stomach, restore your self-confidence, give you a more positive attitude and enable you to face things you've been running away from, for years!"

Moving Forward

Like working out, at first you don't feel the full effects. Sometimes I was still disillusioned with society, so sad about the future for all those women left in a toxic work environment, earning less pay for the same job and losing earned promotions to incompetent males. When the negative thoughts wouldn't leave me, I hung my head and prayed for guidance. It shocked me, nearly knocking me over when help came right away, the Voice, again, inside my head (God? a Higher Power? the Universe? my own subconscious?) instructing me: *Go for a walk.*

After losing my job I had been so depressed it was hard to get out of bed. How the hell was I to go for a walk when I couldn't even get dressed, take a shower, or get off the couch? I had been living in my sweats, and my next thought, or Voice, prompted me to just slip on my clumsy Ugg boots, walk to the door, and open the door, walk down the short flight of stairs, through the small parking lot, and to the mailbox.

Because I wanted to shut up the now-nagging voice and I also wanted to put off looking for a job, I grabbed my house keys, shoved on the boots, and for some reason picked up my wallet and clomped down the stairs. My body screamed, *Turn back.* Wheel of Fortune *is on; let's just watch it for a little bit, take a small nap first, and then we'll go for a walk.*

Usually this worked, but surprisingly I quickly countered with, *All we have to do is walk to the mailbox, and then you can do anything you want and eat anything you want.* The promise of a "fix" of something fattening and sugary must have flooded my brain with endorphins because I flew down the stairs and made it to the mailboxes in record time.

For once, it was a beautiful day in Seattle. The sun had come out momentarily, and although it was still drizzling, little warm rays hit my back, promising a hint of spring. I stretched, turning my pale face upward, breathing deeply, the heavy, achy cloud of despair withdrawing a teeny-tiny bit. As I looked around, small bright-green and yellow and pink buds everywhere copied me, reaching hard for that teasing warmth of a small sunshine patch, tired from the last eight months of gloomy gray rain. When I took a bigger breath through my nose, my lungs filled with the smell of pine, forest muskiness, and, coming from somewhere, my favorite scent—sweet, heavy lilac.

Getting out from under the shadows of the apartments, forcing heavy legs and sluggish limbs, finally feeling a bit of life awakening inside myself, I didn't hesitate when I reached the sidewalk and fixated on my goal, just a little farther down, the main road to our apartment club house.

How It All Started

The books said that all I had to do was picture the end result I wanted, and then the right people and opportunities would come my way. It was very difficult at first to keep images of being successful when the reality of not having a job and being in debt was staring at me daily, but as I practiced seeing my end results, I got better and better at it. When I was first called to answer an ad that was direct mailed to me on a health/weight loss product, the guy who placed the ad said to me, "How fat are you?" I was so stunned; I just hung up on him. **That guy today has lost millions because he didn't know how to answer the phone.**

A short time later, I responded to another ad that was under "Help Wanted" in the local paper that said: "We pay you to lose weight. $1,700 to $4,000 per month full time and part time positions."

"I'm calling about your ad," I asked, hopeful that he would be professional.

"Can I have your name please?"

This threw me off because I didn't want to give out my personal information until I knew what this was all about. I stuttered, "I'm… I'm…c-calling about your ad. I. Just. Want. Some. Information."

"And I would just like your name."

Speechless, embarrassed to tell him who the fat girl was that was calling until I knew who he was and what the job entailed, I just sat there.

He finally said, "Well, I'll tell you my name then. My name is Dave, what is your name?"

"Uh…my name is Sarah," I stumbled, saying the first fake name that came to me, not understanding why I was lying.

"Sarah, do you have a last name?"

Why didn't he just tell me about the job?

"Look, I'm calling for some information about the job you have advertised. I just want some information about your company."

He started laughing at me and meanly asked, "How heavy are you?"

Didn't he understand how difficult it was for someone who knows they need to lose weight to jump right in and start telling a stranger how they let themselves go? Didn't he realize the amount of courage that same person needed to have to admit that they have hit such a low in their life, that they have to be calling someone like him?

Why didn't they have someone answering the phones that had been overweight and wasn't so condescending? Slamming the phone down wasn't good enough, and I picked it up and slammed it twice more. That guy would also lose millions of dollars again because he didn't understand "Basic Marketing."

Opening another paper, I saw the same ad with a different number. This time I heard, "Hi, this is John. Can I help you?"

"Yes. Have you hired the twenty-nine people yet for losing weight?"

"No, we haven't. Are you interested?"

"How many positions do you have left?"

Faltering, he paused and then answered, "Uh…we have… twenty-one positions left."

"Can you tell me a little bit about your company?"

"Sure. What is your name?"

Frustrated, angry, each word clipped, I said again, "Can you just please tell me about your company!"

"We are a fifteen-year-old nutritional company and do business in forty-five different countries."

Finally! "Great. How much are you paying?"

"Well," he stammered, "how many pounds do you want to lose?"

Why couldn't he just tell me how much the position paid? Embarrassed, I answered, stiffly, "Fifty."

"Okay." He seemed relieved. "What is your name and address?"

What the hell is going on? What kind of company asked questions like this? Shouldn't there be an interview? Was there even a position available? Wasn't this illegal?

"Can. You," I demanded, saying each word slowly, "Please. Tell me *how* I get paid to lose weight?"

Silence and then, "Well, we set up an appointment with you, and you come down and meet us—"

I cut him off, furious now. "Why won't you tell me how much this job pays?"

Finally, embarrassed, he said, "Our packages start at two hundred dollars and—"

"I'm calling about a job to lose weight and you want me to pay you two hundred dollars?!" I shouted. "Don't you think if I had two hundred dollars, I wouldn't be calling you asking for a job?" Unbelievable! What a scam. How could they do this to people who needed to lose weight and wanted to work?

"Once you start taking the product and you lose weight, you'll be able to sell it to your friends and family," he hurriedly read from a script.

"Greaaa-at," I said, sarcastically drawing out the word. "And your product, does it really work?"

"Absolutely!" he exclaimed. Excited now, he rolled into his canned pitch. "We've had thousands lose weight and are now making ten thousand dollars a month!"

Come on! What kind of scam was this? "Then how about *you* give me your product, and when I lose the weight, I'll start selling it and pay you back the two hundred dollars?"

"We don't do it that way."

"If you really believe in this product and if you are really making ten grand a month, then why wouldn't you?"

Silence.

Angrily, I answered for him, "Of course you don't do business this way. You. Are. A. Scam. Someone who goes after people who are at their worse and have nowhere else to go."

Smashing the phone back into the cradle again, I starting crying, ashamed of myself—ashamed that I had let myself go, ashamed that I was so stupid thinking that there might be a company out there that would really help someone like me.

Weeks went by and I called another weight loss ad that was mailed to my home. It came in an envelope with a bunch of other flyers for laundry service, local restaurants, cable service, etc. It said that the product was money back guaranteed, cost $30, and came with "free samples." I thought to myself, *Now or never.*

I called, but I kept getting an answering machine that didn't give me any information. I hung up three times over the next two days. Finally I left my name and number. After a week went by, I saw the same ad in the local paper and decided to call it.

"Lose weight, feel great. This is Linda."

"Hi, I'm calling about your ad and your free samples."

"Great! I lost eight pounds in two weeks. It's one hundred percent natural, thirty dollars, and has a money-back guarantee. I can take your credit card information and you can get it in the mail in just a few days, or you can come by." I didn't have a credit card, so she told me if I would put a check in the mail today, she would send out the product. She had made it easy. I also learned what an effective sale looked like that day.

Lessons Learned and Shared

Learn how to answer your phone correctly. Understand that the second you start talking, you are training that person. If you don't make it simple, fun, and easy, that person will think they can never do what you are doing. Tell your success story first. Talk about what your product has done for you and your loved ones.

Identify with the person. Know success stories of truckers, wait-resses, single mothers, professionals. Sell and advertise a low-cost product to get your foot in the door, then listen to the person and plant a seed of upgrades, referrals, and working with you WHEN they get a product result.

CHAPTER 3

My Journey

I began to use my supply of herbs, and I could feel the little tablets kicking in right away, that hour, feeding my brain, nourishing my starved body. As I started to feel better, I began to remember all the things that I had pushed aside and had actually done really well at.

My inner voice was saying to me, ***You were picked out of 15,000 people and made it on*** Wheel of Fortune! ***YOU WON $33,300, beating the best competitors nationwide, at the lowest time in life. You started an "all girl" trucking company and you bought and owned 2 houses before you were 22! You got yourself and your husband hired at Boeing when they weren't even hiring. You attended classes every night after working 8-hour shifts and weekends at Boeing. You did all that!***

Instead of sleeping in, depressed, I was jumping out of bed early, doing the Rocky dance, and that morning I jammed on my sweats, and for the first time in a long time, I walked the two miles to the gym.

Down the Rabbit Hole

Because I couldn't afford to buy the books that would teach me HOW, I lived at the library and began reading up on the 21 different herbs that were in the pills I was taking. I researched each one and became excited when I found out one of the herbs, Valerian, helped depression. Some of the other herbs were diuretics, and two or three were stimulants. There seemed to be a lot of controversy on the main ingredient, ma huang, but I didn't care. I felt great, and after losing 4 lbs. my first week, I had lost 5 more the next week, and coming up on my third week, I ran out. After squirreling away the $36 I need, thanks to not buying junk food and beer at the grocery store, I called Linda up and agreed to drive over to her house to pick them up so I could get them that day.

Normally, I would have hated to leave my apartment to go anywhere, but I was feeling so good it didn't bother me, and I was turning into her neighborhood a half hour later. Looking up from my driving notes, I pulled over, thinking I had taken a wrong turn somewhere. The homes were beautiful, in the $300,000 range, big money for me at the time, and I drove back to the nearest strip mall to find a telephone booth and called her.

Agoraphobia Saved My Life

She explained that I had been in the right place, to just keep going until the end and her house would be close to the woods, on the left. Understanding now that she lived just beyond the gated homes, I got back into my rat-trap Honda and tried not to be embarrassed as I drove by these wonderful homes, hoping that no one would notice the dents in each side and the smoke coming out of the broken tail pipe.

Reaching the end of the instructions, I looked up and just stared. Her house was one of the biggest and prettiest houses on the block. I held my breath as I rang the doorbell, thinking I was still at the wrong house.

As the door opened and I saw Linda for the first time, I backed away, ready to apologize to the heavy, barely dressed woman who answered. Her hair was frizzy and unkempt, and her house slippers were ratty. It was one o'clock in the afternoon, and it looked like she had just woken up.

"You must be Chris. Come in," she said, opening the door just enough to let me through. I followed her through the house, wondering why it was so dark, and without thinking, I said, "Is your power out?"

When she said, "I'm bulimic and an agoraphobic too," I almost bolted, remembering that I hadn't told anyone where I was going, but calmed down when we entered the gorgeous kitchen.

Never Judge a Book by Its Cover

We sat down and I rudely blurted, "I thought you told me that these products were incredible and that you had lost weight." If she had lied to me about how great this whole thing was and how much money she made and if it didn't really work, it would break me. If she took away the little bit of hope I did have that this product would help me…

"I lost over seventy pounds and my allergies cleared up, my bulimia is cleared up, and I'm losing more each week."

"Didn't you tell me you had been in this company for five years?" I asked warily.

"Yes, but this new Thermogenics product just came out two months ago and people are losing weight like crazy."

I didn't want to leave without my pills, so I handed her my $36 and she gave me back $4 since she didn't have to ship it to me.

"You know, we have a lot more products, weight-loss tea, protein shakes…"

"Just the pills, please," I said firmly.

"I'll put in a few samples of the NRG tea and the shake mix." I watched her put a bunch of literature and the samples in a bag. As she did this, she handed me what looked like a check.

I read, "$5,000," and asked, "What's this?"

"It's what I made last month," she answered slyly.

"Whaa-whaat, from selling these pills?" I felt dizzy.

Handing me an even bigger readout, she said, "I use to make over ten thousanad a month, before the United States Senate made us relabel our packaging."

I stared at the $10,000 checks from the last years, looked at Linda, and then around the house. I noticed a picture of her in front of a plane. She caught where my eyes had landed.

"I learned how to fly and bought a plane," she said casually.

Sitting there, I started to shake and got really excited. If this lady could earn that kind of money, with all her problems—she couldn't even leave her house for goodness sake—I would get rich.

Lessons Learned and Shared

Utilize FREE SAMPLES! In all your advertising and business cards. Give samples that the person can feel instantly.

SHOW your success. If you don't have any yet, show your colleagues' checks. I used dozens of $30 checks to show my customers who had experienced success to entice them into registering with the company under me.

CHAPTER 4

Becoming the "$79" Millionaire

After using the products, for the first time in my entire life, I had no trouble getting out of bed. The pounding of my heart startled me awake; my eyes flew open and I jumped out of bed, heading for the bathroom.

I met my eyes in the mirror and felt a rush in my solar plexus.

"OMG, this stuff works!" I yelled out loud.

A huge grin filled the mirror, but before I could admire it, my old self filled my thoughts. *You just think it is working because you want it to so much.*

Doubts flooded my thoughts, taking over the weaker, newer good thoughts, and reminded me of the thousands of studies I had read about placebos given in the war when the medics had run out of morphine.

Wounded and dying soldiers swallowing fake pills, with nothing but sugar in them and instantly feeling high, unable to feel the doctors slicing, stitching their bodies... The mind is so powerful, but who cared as long as it worked?

Taking the pills two times a day at 10 a.m. and 3 p.m. didn't work for me. They gave me so much energy that I couldn't sleep at night, so I set my alarm for 5 a.m., put four green and two beige out with a glass of water, and barely hearing the alarm, I downed the pills in my sleep. At 7 a.m. my eyes flew open and I immediately threw off the covers and got up! Feeling great, I found myself putting my stuff away that I had left on the floor, thrown in a closet, and stuffed under the couch, and by the time my husband came in the door 45 minutes later, instead of looking like a bomb had gone off, the apartment was inviting, welcoming, and breakfast—scrambled eggs with turkey meat—was ready.

"Are you okay? I mean…the place… It looks like you're feeling better?"

Laughing nervously, I replied, "I think so." I didn't want to tell him about the pills yet, because I was afraid he would get mad about the money or—even worse—make fun of the whole thing.

He was still working midnight to seven, and as he got ready for bed, I got into the shower and he called through the door, "You're not going to come lay down with me?" Since I had been fired, he found me sound asleep every morning when he got off work, and I'd usually be there until ten or eleven, when I would get up and go lay down on the couch and watch TV.

"I'm going to go see Mom today and go for a walk," I said.

I could tell he was excited, hoping that the new me would last but afraid to say anything in case it knocked me back to where I had been for the last year.

How I Became the "$79" Millionaire

Linda explained to me if I registered with the company, I could buy my pills at wholesale. I called my father and asked to borrow his credit card for a purchase of $79. Dad didn't mind loaning any of us money, but he made us sign a contract so there would never be any misunderstandings and to teach us to always do that in life.

"Dad, I'm taking this vitamin product that is really making me feel better—I've already lost twelve pounds. I need the money to register with the company so I can buy it wholesale, and you don't have to worry, I am not going to get involved selling this stuff, I just want to get it for wholesale."

We agreed that I would pay it back monthly.

My First 12 Leads

This was my third month taking the pills. I headed back up to Linda's. After we finished the paperwork, she handed me a list of 12 names.

"This is a list of leads that came from the flier you saw, that I couldn't get to. They're kind of old, but you can have them."

I gave her a blank look, not understanding. I knew how she felt: I was worried that it might happen to me again.

Then she said, "I was molested as a child. These products saved my life. I'm so much better than I was."

Back home, I checked to make sure my husband was still sleeping and took the phone to the other end of the apartment. Looking at the names on the list, I realized I didn't know what to say.

I called Linda and she asked me, "Did you go through your registration kit? Everything you need to know is in there."

"Not what to say!" I'd gone through the whole thing, and it was a bunch of junk, with some shake powder and two other bottles of vitamins I didn't need.

"Just say what I said when we first talked."

This infuriated me. "That was a while ago. Don't you have a script or something?"

"A script would make you sound automatic. Just talk to them."

She hung up, and I sat there shaking my head. How had I fallen into this again? I didn't want to do this business and here I was doing it! I wadded the sheet up, ready to throw it away, when I remembered that I had to pay my dad back. I hesitated, then remembered that I had lost 18 pounds in my first three weeks—that was all that mattered! I smoothed out the paper and called the first number.

An older woman answered.

"Hi, I'm returning a call from Edna from the home mailer: 'Lose 30 pounds, 30 days, $30,' my name is Chris."

Silence.

"I know it's been a while since you called—"

Irritably, she broke in and said, "Two months."

"Wow, really? I'm just getting your name and number because the woman that ran the ad is so overwhelmed she couldn't get back to everyone." Not taking a breath, I continued, "I called off this very same ad and I was really skeptical. I had tried everything to lose weight and lost my money on things that didn't work, but this stuff is so incredible that I felt it the first hour—and I lost four pounds my first week, second pounds the second week, then two the next week, then seven pounds the fourth week." I paused. "I had been depressed, I felt awful—couldn't get off the couch—and now I have energy, I feel great, and I look great!"

Taking a breath, I was ready to continue when she interrupted me. "Look, you talk so fast that I don't even know what you just said, but whatever you're on, I'll take it!"

Looking at my reflection in the apartment's big picture window—eyes wide, mouth open—I jumped up and down and did a little dance. I explained to her that I didn't have a merchant account to take her credit card, and she promised to put a check in the mail that day.

My Big Breakthrough

Shaking, I sat back down and called all the people on the list. Out of 12 names I reached 10 people and sold 9! The one I didn't sell was upfront with me that she didn't have the $30. I told her about my life and how low I had been for the last year and said, "If you know three or four people that want to lose weight, you have them call me, and if they buy, I'll mail yours to you for free."

The next day four of her friends called, all buying, and I had to call Linda back to get product to mail out to everyone.

"You sold them all?" she asked, amazed.

"All but the two who weren't at home, but the four referrals I got made up for that." My words were coming out fast, and I felt a thrill at having a product that really worked.

Linda was worried that some of the people wouldn't follow through and send their checks, so she gave me her merchant account number and explained to me how to use it.

"I'll reimburse you each month, after you send me the sales information." She then gave me 15 more leads and asked if I wanted to go put up posters with her. I didn't know what she was talking about, but I said yes and she told me she'd pick me up at midnight.

We drove just a couple of miles, and Linda turned on her blinker, pulling into a Kinko's Copy shop. She had an 8 x 11 master copy of a sign on regular typing paper. "Lose 30 lbs, $30, 30-day guarantee." I added "FREE SAMPLES!" to the top of it, and I was in business.

Lessons Learned and Shared

We all have excuses for why we won't do something. Linda didn't let her problems stop her, and I didn't let mine stop me. Do not give up if you hit obstacles, because you will. We all do.

Don't let not having money to advertise or set up an office stop you.

When you sponsor someone, you are responsible for them. If you don't have the money for advertising, then go out and generate business by following the examples I and many others did. Take those leads and, with the customers who have experienced success with your product, show them how to earn extra income by giving them some leads to get cash in their pocket right away.

Put into them what they are giving to you. Let them know that you believe in them and paint that picture of success for them. **Know their dreams and goals.**

CHAPTER 5

Taking that First Step

How do you move forward? You have to make the choice to take that first step.

I found a business that I really wanted to work. I knew that I wanted to take the fastest road to reaching success, and in picturing what that looked like, I saw myself breaking records and doing things no one else had thought of to reach that goal.

As with any organization, there are the "newbies" and the "veterans." All around me the "veterans" were talking about the road to the top. Their path to capture the glad was laid out and long. Each of them was intent on following a trail that went around and around the mountain in a spiral. The shortest road to any goal is the one that goes straight up. It's harder, but you get there faster. As I looked at their road map, things just didn't add up. Why would you take a road that will guarantee you not make your goals for years?

I didn't want to take ten years to get to the top, and my gut was screaming at me that this was not the way. I could tell immediately that most of these lessons they were teaching would make it take even longer just to get started. Their plans included getting new boots for climbing, shiny gadgets, and cool matching outfits. This eliminated most of us who were just getting started, as we couldn't afford activities and products. These items should have been considered optional, but the trainers made them out to be necessities. Things such as fax and copy machines, computers, fancy letterhead, new desks, just the right pens, and so on were taking precedence over just selling the product.

Couple that with the fact that their road map included unnecessary rest stops (meetings) to catch their breath every few miles. Three times a week we had meetings to discuss having another meeting, and sometimes after the meeting we would go out to dinner to discuss more meetings. These "veterans" had been in the company 15 years and were teaching that we could achieve their level of success—$10,000 a month and more—by talking to ten people a day. There had to be a better way!

On the surface, from an outsider's perspective, it would seem to be a good route. All of this intense and focused preparation seemed very official, but it rang hollow to me. Is it really necessary for us to go through all of this pomp and fanfare just to sell a product? They wanted nothing more than to make me one of them. Yet, all of this preparation without action looked to me as if it would take ten years to find any success. This was unacceptable. Why would anyone choose a route that would take a decade to reach success? This ran completely against my immediate need to get out of debt. Through books and research that I had been doing before I jumped into this business, I knew there was a better way.

Lessons Learned and Shared

What kind of horse do you want to be?

So many teach others how to be a plow horse. Work hard all day with your head down, and in ten years, you will be successful. Why not be a racehorse?! Change the mindset of doing things the same way everyone else does. Instead of calling 10 people a day, I was going to follow a blueprint where I could talk to 10,000 people a day.

> **Change the mindset of doing things the same way everyone else does. Instead of calling 10 people a day, I was going to follow a blueprint where I could talk to 10,000 people a day.**

After charging up $800 of sales on Linda's merchant account, she wouldn't return my calls so I could get paid ($800 was a lot of money to me). Months went by and I was so discouraged I wanted to quit. I called the company to tell them that my upline refused to pay me, and they said that I was an independent distributor and I had to work it out on my own. When you are just starting out and you have big goals, you have to assess what the consequences are of quitting versus staying. I almost quit, but I'm glad I didn't. Imagine if I had. I would have lost the life I have now.

> **Have you had a moment where you just wanted to give up? This was my moment, but I pushed forward and it was worth it. Going the extra few steps when you are on the verge of quitting is where breakthrough happens.**

Have you had a moment where you just wanted to give up? This was my moment, but I pushed forward and it was worth it. Going the extra few steps when you are on the verge of quitting is where breakthrough happens.

CHAPTER 6

Where's the Level Playing Field?

When I got started in network marketing, the environment was the same as it is today. Highly completive, and if you want to succeed, you must dig deep and push forward. I found it difficult to connect with my upline that I knew was making millions. Back then, there were no Skype groups or online webinars, and information about how to succeed was scarce. I had to do a lot of digging in order to find out how and why people in my area were successful, so that I could duplicate their efforts. Not all successful people are forthcoming with how they got there, and unfortunately, I was often met with resistance.

But this never slowed my ambition.

Have you ever had other people try to hold you back? You can't let others determine your success or how you get there. The goal was set. The only path I could see was the one straight up the mountain to reach it. Nothing was going to stop me.

Who's Trying to Cap Your Ambition?

The company I was involved with at the time had already been around 15 years. I lived in Seattle at the time, and the area didn't bring in enough sales to warrant a company-sponsored training—where was the level playing field in that? I couldn't afford the airfare, and it just didn't seem important to the company to sponsor training in areas with lower growth.

How can we grow if the company doesn't invest in us?

If my sponsor didn't hold training sessions and couldn't be reached, then I found myself trying to figure out on my own how to grow. None of the people in my local group were as determined to build this as more than just a part-time gig, and I hadn't seen any one of them as top earners at the national convention. When you hit a roadblock like this, you have two choices: continue down the path someone else carved for you—or create your own. Finding a way to get more training became my goal.

> **When you hit a roadblock like this, you have two choices: continue down the path someone else carved for you—or create your own. Finding a way to get more training became my goal.**

At the convention I learned that there was one other group two hours from me, but still in my area, that was learning marketing skills from one of the highest earners in the company. Perfect! After attending the huge annual convention and believing in the familial words that were shared—"All of us work together!—I decided to attend his meeting, knowing in my heart that everyone in the company was here to help everyone succeed. It would be a perfect chance for me to learn. When we hit a wall with our goals, we have to find ways to break through. I knew this was going to be a game changer.

At the event, I had been spellbound. Sitting in the last row of the huge center, I was watching the screen, because the people onstage looked like ants. The words of the owner and founder of the company sank deep.

"We are your family," he said. "Take a look at the person sitting next to you, that guy or girl is going to be there to help you when you have a bad day. When your family or spouse makes fun of you for trying to reach your dreams, you tell them that there are 1.2 million others realizing their dreams that are just waiting to help you."

It was the final push that I needed. Sometimes you can feel held back by the limitations of what is around you. Don't let the lack of the tools you need keep you from continuing to pursue your goals. You are the one who makes the choice to keep going or fall behind.

* * *

Weeks later I was getting ready to make the drive for the training that I knew was going to be instrumental in me reaching my goals. I borrowed my mother's blazer and skirt, made a sack lunch (because I couldn't afford to eat there), and put my last ten bucks into the gas tank. I didn't overthink it; I had the hope and confidence that I would learn at least one thing that would increase my sales. I drove my beat-up Honda two hours in the snow on bare tires. I knew that I had to be there.

Barely making it on time, I saw the one of the few chairs available, way up in front. I scrambled up the forty or more rows, happy that I would finally be trained. This was exciting because it gave me two good things in a row: I had avoided crashing on the freeway with my bare tires, and now I had snagged a seat so close that I would be able to see and hear everything the speaker had to say. I wouldn't miss anything. I was going to learn how to be a millionaire.

The energy was electric. Settling in, I could hear all the excited conversations buzzing around me: people talking and shouts of, "Hey, you look great!" and, "It's good to see ya. How are, Davy and Jen-Jen?" The realization hit; these people knew each other. Bigger than that, they knew each other really well.

I felt jealous that everyone seemed so close, and for a moment, I regressed back into the little kid who hated the little kid who hated to walk into class late. I chided myself for feeling that way. This wasn't like grammar school, with all eyes staring at you and little boys making teasing remarks because you were late. This company was 15 years old; it would be unrealistic to think that people don't know each other. It would be odd if they didn't. Especially with this being the most successful group in town. In fact, I figured, they would probably be clamoring to help me once they found out how my sponsor had essentially abandoned me.

The Moment I Had Been Waiting For

Have you ever put everything you have into one moment? I had laid it all on the line to come here and get training. When the speaker walked in, a broad grin spread across my face. This was my favorite speaker from the annual convention and now they were here. I felt a weight lift off of my shoulders. I knew it would all be all right. The two-hour drive in the snow with bare tires (worse than bald), my last ten bucks in the gas tank, the borrowed blazer and skirt—it wasn't all for nothing. I was going to leave equipped with the tools and tips I needed to be successful.

I set my lunch bag under my seat. I took out my pens and new notebook, then got my water out of my purse. I put everything within arm's reach. I was going be prepared when it came time to ask questions. This was the moment.

The company promised that if I worked hard, became teachable, and helped others, I would be making seven figures too. This was going to be the man that helps me change my life!

The speaker began, "Before we start…"

I leaned in, concentrating on every word that came out of his mouth. The speaker looked kindly up there under the lights, the platform in front of him, his glasses and slightly balding head shining back at us assuredly. His presence gave off the feeling that if he could make all that money, we could too.

He continued, "Is there anyone here that is not in my organization, but another line?"

Almost knocking over my water, I raised my hand excitedly. I thought to myself, *He already wants to help us! This guy is great. He's going to take time to acknowledge those of us who had come all this way that were not even in his group.*

I saw another hand go up. I almost fist-pumped the air. My first distributor had also shown up. Bouncing in my chair, thrilled that the snow hadn't stopped him either, I waved. A huge smile lit up my whole face. He waved back from the last row on the other side of the enormous room.

The speaker finished, "I'm sorry, but this is a closed meeting. You will have to leave."

All the color drained from my face. I was stunned. Then it flamed a hot red. A mixture of anger, frustration, and embarrassment flooded my body. Shaking so hard my notebook fell, along with all of my pens, I dived down trying to hide myself under the chair. I couldn't see. Tears blinded me.

As I tried to reach two of my pens, the man behind me kicked them at me. Ink marks stained my mother's light grey suit. I was mortified. How could this family company just dismiss us this way?

I felt the entire room staring at me, waiting. I could feel that they were annoyed that they were missing valuable teaching minutes, because of me. The two women, on each side of me, shoved my notebook and water bottle into my hands. Their eyes said everything. They didn't want me there. The speaker stood on the platform, microphone silent, refusing to let me hear any millionaire-making tips. I popped up, wiping my eyes, smearing mascara on the only thing I could find, my poor mother's suit sleeve.

I really am on my own, I thought. *Isn't one person going to stand up and say something?*

These two hundred people in the room were the top earners in the entire company. Didn't any of them remember their first days as a new distributor? What had happened to the words they had applauded and cheered during the convention? "All of us work together!" they had shouted. It had only been a week since they had heard their beloved founder tell us that helping each other would get us to $1 billion in sales.

Lessons Learned and Shared

Finally reaching the exit door, I heard a man clear his throat. I turned around, hopeful. Then I saw he was standing with my brown paper bag held high enough for the people in the far back to see. "You forgot your lunch!" he shouted and tossed it to me.

I stepped out into the cold as the laughter rang in the background. Knowing my one distributor was long gone, I bit down on my lower lip, drawing blood. Getting into the freezing car, I dropped the ignition key twice. I finally got the key in the ignition, and for once my car turned over on the first try. The speakers came to life and the cassette tape filled the air, the founder of the company was talking directly to me.

"Let me tell you—I had a lot of things go wrong for me when I first started in the business…but what would have happened if I had quit the first time somebody was mean to me?" Thousands of feet from the live tape started pounding the floors in unison along with cheers, people knowing they wouldn't be there if he had quit. After all that had happened, would you quit? I knew at that moment that I couldn't. I grabbed my notebook and pen and wrote: "Things I will NEVER do when I am number one. HAVE CLOSED MEETINGS. I will bring everyone with me to success."

CHAPTER 7

My Epiphany

You can't be successful and a quitter. You get to be one or the other. What is your choice? I knew that I wanted to be successful and I decided that I wasn't going to be deterred. With or without my company's help, I was going to make it. I created cheap handwritten posters and hung them everywhere.

With or without my company's help, I was going to make it. I created cheap handwritten posters and hung them everywhere.

My phone was ringing off the hook because everyone wanted to get in on my FREE SAMPLES! "Lose up to 30 lbs, $30, 30-day guarantee."

The money I earned from those signs bought my first ad in my local newspaper. When that ad paid for itself, I kept it there, and even purchased an ad in the city next to it. When that ad paid for itself, I bought ads in newspapers throughout the entire state. I could see that the company I was looking at was strong. Analysts and business professionals had them listed as a top company. I loved their product and 95% of the population needed it! It looked like all conditions were right. Knowing that the top people in the company had been talking to 10 people a day for 15 years, I had to find some way to talk to thousands a day to catch up with them.

How do you talk to thousands of people a day? There are only so many minutes and hours. I decided to make a tape of me making sales and made a video of me telling my story. I then had my people use these tools so we wouldn't get burned out. The beauty of those tools was the fact that they could talk to people while we were sleeping and having family time. They changed the game of having one-on-ones and real meetings.

Success Can Be Found Lurking Anywhere

You can't get anywhere on your own knowledge, so I started reading *Think and Grow Rich*, and all of Wayne Dyer's books. I took several sticky notes, wrote $10,000 a month on each, and put them all around my apartment. The books I was reading shared this common theme: You don't have to know *how* something will come to pass. If you will visualize the desired end result, you will emit the proper vibration that will attract to you the right people and opportunities. My customers were losing weight. I supplied them with leads and put money in their pockets right away. Soon, my organization began to grow, and my monthly checks doubled. I qualified for a top party with the company. I was thrilled. Finally, I would have the opportunity to meet the top performers and millionnaires. I would have a chance to learn how they did it.

I arrived early to the champagne event, but found it difficult to get anyone to talk to me. After a while, I found myself leaning against a wall, watching the others mingle. That's when I noticed Bob Anderson was standing right next to me. I introduced myself.

"Hi, I'm new here. I made my first cut of president's team ($10,000 royalties) in just my tenth month retailing."

He introduced himself and said, "I just made fully qualified president's team in my twelfth month recruiting."

I shared with him the retailing methods my group was using, and he invited me to fly in and teach his group. In return, he would teach me how his group was recruiting.

He was amazed at the marketing tools I was bringing to the table. He had never used them himself, but he could see the potential.

Not Everyone Is Going to Get It

When the day came, my team and I approached the group of company veterans, the same group that had set themselves up as "preparation" experts for the past fifteen years. Thus far, they had only modest success to show for their efforts. As a gesture of good faith, and willingness to collaborate, we showed them our new techniques and volunteered to teach them. The proposal we presented to them was simple:

"Why don't we take all of your great ideas, incorporate these new tools we invented, which are already proven, and together we can build a chairlift that will take us straight up the side of the mountain? We can get there faster and have fun doing it."

I felt that there was no time to waste. The mountain was steep, and there would be some hard days ahead, but all the conditions were perfect. We needed to start *immediately*. Everyone had to understand that the gravy train could come to an end. Who knew when there might be a competing company right behind us? I tried to get them to understand that though we may not be able to see into the future, or know what may await us around the next bend in the road, the flag at the top of the mountain was attainable *right now*. All that was needed was for us to work together as a team. There was no need to take the slow and laborious way up the mountain, plodding along like pack mules. We wanted to run like racehorses.

Not Everyone Wants to Be a Racehorse

Sadly, the group got really mad that we wanted to change things. They couldn't grasp the fact that we were giving them a chairlift ride up the mountain, instead of hiking up the long way. They were used to thinking a certain way, and no matter how brilliant our plan was, they simply would not accept it. They thought we were insane. They were mad at us for challenging their expertise by introducing new ideas. They not only turned their backs on us; they told everyone to throw snowballs at us.

They took it one step further and brought in the big guns to slow us down. Lawyers. Instead of focusing their energy on selling product and making money, their sole objective had become to knock us over and bruise us so we couldn't climb. For the most part, it was really sad, but our small group wrapped our arms around each other and resolved to take advantage of the new opportunity before us.

Lessons Learned and Shared

Help your neighbor and the rewards will come back to you tenfold. Enough said. Why not be a racehorse? To this day I hear speakers teaching the theory that your journey to success should be like that of a packhorse.

"Just stay on the path, be diligent."

"This is not a sprint, it is a marathon."

You don't have to follow that plan! You can have success now! You can learn and earn at the same time. What you focus on, what you believe and think, is what will happen.

CHAPTER 8

Taking the Mountain

I saw early on that any business you decide to go into is like a mountain. "Success" would be the flag at the top of that mountain. Sometimes, you are going to climb the mountain by yourself, but usually you will have partners, as well as colleagues that have been in that business for a while. Franchises are a good example, but it applies to most any business. Real estate offices, car dealerships, network marketers—again, nearly any businesses you can think of—will have someone showing you the ropes.

The Nature of Success

Picture yourself at the bottom of a mountain, looking way up at the flag on the peak. The bodies of all who have gone before you, and did not make it, are strewn up and down the side of the mountain. You and your team share the same goal. Get to the top.

There are many different ways you can get to the top. You could follow the footsteps of the people that have gone before you, but what if you knew that it had taken them ten years, or more, just to reach the halfway point? Would you want to take the same the route? You could mortgage your home, sell everything you have, and get as many credit cards as you can just to buy a vehicle to get you up there. Many do that, but is that what you want? There will be salespeople everywhere trying to sell you magic hiking boots, a ride on a group bus with special wheels that are on order, even special wings that would allow you to fly to the top of the mountain. The options are seemingly endless. Which way is the best way?

Only you can answer that question for yourself. You have to find the path that fits you and you must be willing to look at the advice you are given for exactly what it is worth. If someone is on a ten-year plan, it may not be for you, particularly if you are on a two- or three-year plan.

Lessons Learned and Shared

Before you take the advice of anyone, **ask to see their check** and **find out how long they have been in the company.**

If they aren't willing to show you their check, do *not* follow their plan.

CHAPTER 9

Know Your Worth

As I overcame obstacles and began developing real success, others would reach out to me for advice. Sometimes they were in my downline and sometimes they were not. One such person, we will call her Debbie, was a school teacher. She was a wonderful lady and I helped her build her new business.

Real Success Requires Unconventional Thinking

Debby had received a phone call from a local Seattle radio station asking her if she'd be interested in buying "air time." The radio sales rep had seen a small ad of Cindy's that I had given her. The ad read, "WILLPOWER in a Bottle. Lose weight feel great. FREE SAMPLES! $-back guarantee." It was an ad that worked for Cindy right away, but didn't cost her a lot of money.

I advised Debby to call the rep back and say, "Sure, if you buy my product, I might be interested in buying air time." The salesperson agreed, but didn't have the money for Cindy's product, so they bartered. Cindy let the rep try the product for free, and the rep got Cindy's product mentioned on air for free. The on-air mention of Cindy's product generated enough sales to pay for more ads, and the rep began selling Cindy's product!

Not a One-Time Fluke

This kind of bartering, "product for advertising," wasn't just a one-time fluke. A newscaster on one of Seattle's morning television shows saw a poster that had been put up by another one of my team members. We will call her Alice. Alice was just starting out. She was a single mother of two, lived in an apartment in a drug-infested neighborhood, and didn't have a lot of money to start her business.

We had made posters that we stapled to telephone poles at major intersections throughout the city. (Check to see if this is legal in your city.) The reporter flashed a shot of the poster on television, and Alice's phone number was put out on the morning, noon, and nightly news. Her phone rang off the hook. The reporter actually said, on television, that she didn't believe the product would work. We called her up and told her it did. The reporter agreed to try her product on air to see if it was what it claimed to be.

The reporter went back on air to say that she would try Alice's product and then get back to viewers in two weeks. Alice's phones went insane. I stopped by her drab apartment and she was crying. She couldn't handle all of the calls she was receiving from people ready to buy! I laughed until I nearly cried, and we proceeded to turn Alice's fifteen minutes of fame into over $5,000 a month. About four months later I was helping her move out of that horrible apartment and into her first home.

Where There's a Will...

We repeated the technique of bartering for ads in other states as well. Another lady was asked to sponsor her friend in a charity walk-a-thon. She didn't have any money to sponsor her friend, but made a deal with her. If her friend agreed to wear some advertising during the walk-a-thon, she would donate a portion of any sakes she received. Her friend agreed. They actually handwrote an ad on the back of a T-shirt! There were thousands of people attending that walk, including news crews and reporters. Both ladies benefited from the sales that were generated as a result.

I have another friend who recently purchased a valet service for high-end restaurants in Palm Beach. He has a friend who owns a limo company, and this friend asked him to hand out business cards to patrons of the restaurants he serviced who might have had too much to drink. He agreed to do so if, in return, the owner of the limo company told his clients about the valet service for when they had private parties at their million-dollar mansions.

Everyone You Are Buying from Should Be Buying from You

Think about how often you buy something, or are approached to buy something. What if all of the people you are buying from started buying from you? Would that be life changing?

I have a friend who barters her product with her maid, gardener, pool person, hairdresser, nail technician, and even her doorman. She refuses to do business with anyone unless they do business with her. What happens if they don't want your product? Find someone who will! She went through four hairdressers until she found one who would do her hair in return for free product.

You may not think you have a service with which you can barter, but I bet you do. I've shown Realtors how to use this concept, as well as printers, car salesmen, and lawyers. The list goes on and on. Now, think about your grandma, parents, friends, and neighbors. All of them are buying, or being asked to buy something.

In fact, isn't most everyone you going to need to buy a new television, car, house, furniture, or computer sooner or later? Nearly all of those businesses involve a salesperson who could be buying from you. These are just a few ideas you can use to generate more business, regardless of what business you are in.

Lessons Learned and Shared

My favorite advice to give has always been: "If you treat your business like a million-dollar business, it will respond like one!" When in doubt about how to proceed in your marketing, do what the big guys do. Follow the business that has the biggest check, and please don't miss this, in the shortest amount of time.

If someone is teaching you to talk to people one-on-one, ask them how long they have been in the business. If they tell you thirty years, then imitate that person only if you want to take thirty years to succeed!

There is always room for improvement regardless of the tools you use. There is nothing wrong with coming up with a great new idea that you believe is better than the one making you millions a year. Just use the same rule as all big companies do: **Test it before you release it. Add to your momentum. Don't stop that money-making machine. Keep it going while you test a new one.**

CHAPTER 10

Where Are They Now?

I mentioned before how, early in my network marketing life, two different groups turned their backs on me. One group attempted to humiliate me, the other ignored me and then actively worked against me. You may have experienced something similar on your journey. Sometimes, the challenges may come from well-meaning friends attempting to give you unsolicited advice.

I combined my retailing ideas with what Bob Anderson was doing to achieve fast results, and we both got a rocket ride to the top. I took all of the knowledge I had obtained from studying books on marketing, advertising, and sales and taught his group how to retail, get upgrades and massive referrals, and turn their leads into customers for life.

Gift Horse Sabotage

I experienced more pain from people trying to hold me back than I did by going straight up that mountain! That's okay. I brought just six of my salespeople with me, and from that six I created an income of over $100,000 a month in about fourteen. We implemented our techniques, and it did all of the work for us. That chairlift up the mountain actually turned into a rocket, and the people who tried to hold us back ended up stuck on the side of the mountain, plodding along with their pack mule attitudes.

Ten More Years of Preparation

Ten years after my initial success, I decided to check up on my old "veteran" friends. Sadly, I discovered that many of them were in the same place they were at ten years before. The entire group still had not made it, and they even lost some people along the way. In other words, many of the so-called "veterans" had fallen and rolled back down the mountain. Some had even been pushed down by their own partners that were climbing next to them!

The Silver Lining

Do I feel vindicated? Heck no. I truly wanted to be part of the group that had been around me early on. They say it's lonely at the top, and for me it was. I took nice vacations and attended great parties, but I there was a void within me. All the while I kept following my marketing rules and making money. Eventually, the veterans group and I made amends. I called them up one day to share my marketing blueprint. I encouraged them to copy it, and they finally did.

CHALLENGE 1: 28-Day Challenge to Blossom Your Ambition

If you have ever wished for a day when someone would come along and help you achieve a better life, that day has come. If you will commit to adopting the following habits for 28 days, your life will change forever.

Allow me to reiterate.

Your. Life. Will. Change. Forever.

Do you understand? It doesn't matter if you believe me or not. If you went to the gym every day for 28 days, and did exactly what your trainer told you to do, your body would transform. The same is true for your life if you will commit to implementing the habits I am about to share with you.

This challenge is for everyone. This is for millions of people who say that they want to stop working frantically, and stressfully, and for 70 hours a week.

I have NEVER had anyone tell me that they followed through with these steps and didn't reach their goals. NEVER. I have had people who quit after 28 days and end up right back where they started, but no one who adopted these habits for life has ever ceased to grow and expand.

These daily habits are as important for your life as drinking water is for your body. If you stop, and you go back to focusing on everything that is wrong with the world, your thoughts will begin sending different signals to your cells and will adversely affect your health.

You will attract into your life whatever you are focusing your attention on. Why not be the one-half of one percent that enjoys life and have the excitement and energy to live it to its fullest?

Embrace this 28-Day Challenge and Let The Changes Begin!

1. Stop watching television and silly videos on the internet. You don't have to worry that you will miss something important because there will be plenty of people around you to tell you about all the gloom and doom. Instead, educate and motivate yourself by reading a book, listening to an uplifting podcast, or watching a motivational video. Whatever your mode of learning is, use it to expand and strengthen yourself. If your spouse or family members complain, put earphones on or go into another room.

2. When you wake up in the morning, and before you get out of bed, visualize your entire day going great. See yourself, in vivid detail, where you want to be in a month, two months, and in a year. Picture the new car

you in your driveway, your family's needs fulfilled, and your wardrobe filled with the kind of clothes you've always wanted. Visualize your new office and taking your dream vacation.

3. Listen to something motivational, such as a CD or MP3, while you are getting ready in the morning, preparing your breakfast, or driving to work. If your family isn't willing to help you, picture in your mind them sitting around the breakfast table listening and talking about the CD that will change their future.

4. Your loved ones will notice the changes in you. They will see you becoming happier, healthier, and will want to experience the same. They will decide to give the 28-Day Challenge a try as well. When this happens, you will see something phenomenal take place. As the people around you become involved, the positive energy in your household will be amplified. When you have more minds working together, you become more powerful and success comes faster.

5. Wherever you are during the day, take a break and re-energize your mind. In the same way that you need to eat food to fuel your body, you will need to refuel your mind as well. Maybe you were in a meeting where everything was negative, or you let your co-worker talk at length about everything bad in her life, or maybe you joined in and told her stories about how bad your life was. STOP. You must choose to stop and say, "Let's talk about what is good in our life."

Lessons Learned and Shared

Focus on all of the good in your life. Your health, loved ones, and even your job. You may not love your job, but it is still better than not having one. If you don't have a job, then look for anything that you are thankful for. If your list is short, focus your thoughts and conversation on what you want to have. Be specific and let your words create a picture. Talk in detail about the perfect spouse, career, or business you want to have. **Fill your mind with anything and everything that makes you feel good.**

> **"We have proven that space and time are not conditions in which we live; they are modes in which we think. What we see depends upon the theories we use to interpret our observations."**
>
> **NOTE FROM ALBERT EINSTEIN'S DIARY**

CHAPTER 11

My First Successful Business

When I was a child, I was always coming up with ways to make money. I learned about network marketing by selling walnuts and getting others involved in my success. As I grew older, the entrepreneurial spirit never left me, but like all young people I had multiple odd jobs in order to make ends meet. One such job was a waitress. However, unlike many people, I didn't view being a waitress as a job. I saw it as a business.

Operating My Waitress Business

Being a waitress was the first business I was involved in that I became a success at. There are millions of waitresses and waiters around the world. Oftentimes, they are taken for granted. They are the invisible workforce that day in and day out interacts with customers face-to-face. Yet, few people stop to ask themselves, *What is a waitress?*

The answer is simple. They are service people. If they are good and effective at their job, they are the key to a restaurant operating at 100%. They are the restaurant's "salespeople."

Few people truly understand everything that goes on in the restaurant business. They come in, look at the menu, order, have their meal, and leave. Behind the scenes there are quotas for wait staff (i.e. sales force), and there are contests for promoting different items. Management informs the wait staff what items need to be sold immediately, and the value of every plate of food is known down to the penny. Don't forget the tip. This is just one form of the total commissions that go back to the sales force, better known as the wait staff.

Working as a waitress opened my eyes to the inner workings of this mechanism. I quickly realized that my job was a business, and that I had an opportunity to make as much as I want, within reason of course, if I approached this with my focus on the customer.

The Onion Ring Loaf Contest

I remember one month when we had a contest going on who could sell the most onion ring loaf appetizers. The restaurant I was working for did these promotions often and was always keen on giving recognition to successful service people. They also handed out bonuses. This made me excited and the competitive side of me kicked in instantly. At the same time the contest was going on, the restaurant had gotten a great deal on a white wine. So the contest rules were simple: who ever could sell the most appetizers got a bottle of wine and a free dinner.

This was a win-win for the restaurant. They moved more onion ring loaf appetizers, and the bonus they gave us (white wine) was something they were received at less than wholesale prices anyway, and the dinner was at cost.

The contest lasted for a month, and I won nearly every night by following a simple formula. This formula can and should be implemented in every business. I later applied the exact same formula to another contest at the restaurant, and eventually used it to become successful in network marketing.

My Waitress Business Formula

When my customer was seated, I acknowledged them with a friendly greeting, and then proceeded to plant a seed, limit their choices, share a a testimonial, and create urgency. I did all of that in less than two minutes.

Example:

- I greeted them, found something positive to say about how they looked, their children, etc. (recognition, acknowledgment).
- I then told them in detail, how our number one appetizer and wine special was incredible (planted a seed, limited choices).
- I used basic sales and advertising skills by using words like, "everyone" (testimonial).
- "One of our most popular appetizers. Everyone that tried it loves it. Sometimes we even run out." That last phrase increased my sales significantly (created urgency).

Keep Your Integrity

Now, understand that these phrases were all true, but they could have been applied to any of our appetizers. There were at least six or seven other appetizers for them to choose from, and they were all very good and popular.

Yet, I could see that the customers almost always went with the wine or appetizer that I suggested. The reason for that was the formula I was using. Every time that I won the contest, I gained more confidence. I was a new employee and didn't get the same respect the other employees had earned from being there so long. It was the only leveling tool that helped me get noticed by the manager and the owners.

As a result of this contest, and many more, I ended up being assigned to the best shifts. I essentially got to pick my own hours, and most importantly, I became recognized by my peers as a wonderful waitress. The same "recognition" that I was giving, was now being given to me. It felt really good to come into work each night.

My tips (commissions) were higher than everyone else, every night I worked. I was then tasked with teaching the other wait staff the formula I had created. As a result, the restaurant made more money, and the top wait staff began to help me and treat me as one of their own.

Lessons Learned and Shared

No matter where you are in life, you can apply basic marketing strategies.

Remember, you are always selling. You sell yourself to your boss, spouse, children, and so on. It's important that you develop these skills, and doing so will improve all of your relationships. Business and personal.

Read books on marketing and advertising. If you only learn one thing, your business and life will be magnified.

Pay attention to advertising that is mailed to your home. I ordered a swim suit from Victoria's Secret twenty years ago, and I still get a catalog in the mail.

Think about what makes you want to buy something. Incorporate that strategy into what you are doing.

When you add words like "Free Samples" and "Money Back Guarantee" to your advertising or business cards, you will attract more business.

CHAPTER 12

Copying the Success Blueprint

I still smile when I think about the first time my dad saw my mansion in Malibu. The man who had lent me $79 to begin my journey into network marketing was finally going to see what his seed had sown.

My dad, a lifelong factory worker for Boeing, looked around in amazement. His eyes widened as he watched the majestic gates rolling open. I clearly remember him and my mom climbing up the steps to enter the house. Zuma Beach was sparkling brightly in the background. I saw his eyes dart across the three-acre lot, taking in the putting green, sand trap, two-story artist's cottage, guest house, and finally the main house.

He blurted out, "Are you sure you can afford this?"

Mom told me that night, "Your dad freaked out when we pulled in and begged me to stop pretending, thinking I had the driver pull in to someone else's place!" She was talking so fast. She waved her arms in the air, mimicking Dad shaking his head, eyes narrowed, stating, "I don't believe you."

My dad and grandfathers are gone now, but their values aren't. The work ethic, drive, and the unwavering belief that if you are "paid a dollar, you work a dollar" have been instilled in me. I applied all of those same ethics into my success blueprint to make network marketing work for me. Most importantly, I intentionally did not reinvent the wheel. I focused on perfecting the success blueprint for my industry.

Work Smarter, Not Harder

As a kid, whenever we drove past million-dollar homes, I wondered how those people had become so successful. Why them and not us? My father told me that "those people" had two and even three homes just as magnificent.

I wanted to jump out of the car, run up, and ring their doorbell and ask them how they became so wealthy. Were they smarter than us? Luckier? Did they work harder? Had they inherited their money? Finally, at age 33, I figured it out. They just knew more than I did.

It made sense to me, that if I could learn how they had become so successful and applied those same principles, I could do the same. It's no secret that throughout the ages, success blueprints have been left behind for anyone that sincerely seeks them.

Behind every billion-dollar company there is first a start-up, and in order to achieve the same level of success, all we have to do is copy their success.

Good Marketing Is for Everyone

No matter what job, career, or position you have right now, your first step in getting where you want to go is learning how to deliberately market yourself. Waitresses, doctors, lawyers, managers, house cleaners, actresses, singers, executives—even owners of corporations—all have to deliberately and intentionally market themselves. That is, if they desire to increase their income and business.

Regardless of your present situation, if you will learn how to market yourself you will change your future, and the sooner you apply what you learn, the sooner those changes will occur.

Approach your business, or job, exactly like the billion-dollar companies that create the products you buy every day. When you emulate them, you will achieve the same, if not better results. There is a proven science behind their success. Use it.

Microsoft, Dell, McDonald's—the list is endless. And you can give yourself a competitive advantage that no one else has if you will follow their examples. All successful companies use the same success blueprint that they started with, and they continue using it for decades. Why? Because it works.

When the blueprint is ignored, people lose money, miss promotions, salary increases, opportunities, and repeat business. Oftentimes, instead of copying what has already proven to work, they go off on their own and leave the success blueprint behind. This is a tragedy because it means that they will never achieve their goals and dreams for their life.

Developing the Success Blueprint

It is unfortunate how neglected public libraries are these days. With the explosion of the internet, library hours have been cut around the nation. In ancient times libraries were revered. Not just anyone could enter the "Temple of Knowledge" and check out the scrolls. Today, most anyone can get a free library card and check out as many books as they want. Yet, libraries are largely underutilized.

When I was first starting out, I didn't have the money to buy motivational tapes, books, or movies. The library was my only resource, and it can be that for anyone with a thirst for knowledge. When you cannot afford to go to a bookstore and buy all the books you want or need, the library is there to give you the wisdom for free. Whether you buy books or check them out from the library, when you begin to study motivators and successful people you begin to see that there is clearly a success blueprint at play. Luck can only account for a small fraction of their success, particularly when that success has been sustained for decades.

Tapping into the Success Blueprint

Every successful person I have ever met, especially Donald Trump, whom I got to know well, utilizes a success blueprint daily. As part of manifesting my own success blueprint, I was the only single female under 40 to join both of Donald Trump's exclusive clubs in Palm Beach. In fact, he went out of his way to welcome me and would introduce me to famous people. He was my mentor during that time and was so much fun. All of that manifested in my life because of my self-belief.

Success always begins with an unwavering belief in yourself. If you have ever seen or heard Donald Trump interviewed, he constantly lets everyone know, "I am the greatest," and, "My product is the best."

Muhammad Ali was notorious for incorporating this as part of his success blueprint. Politicians utilize this in their success blueprint. Oprah demonstrates this wonderfully. The reality of the success blueprint is that you must first successfully market yourself to yourself. When you can do that, others will also believe in what you are selling. You must understand that at all times you are marketing yourself. If you don't believe in you, then who will?

You do not need to be vocal when first incorporating this into your success blueprint. However, keep in mind that Muhammad Ali and Donald Trump use this component of the success blueprint *before* they became visibly successful. It's safe to say that if they had they not implemented this kind of self-marketing, they never would have gotten to where they are today.

You see, when you are self-marketing, you must visualize what you want your end result to be. Then focus on that every hour of every day. This will reinforce the success blueprint.

I'll guarantee you that when Donald sets out to open a new multi-billion-dollar show, or a new golf course, he forms a picture of it in his mind's eye. He talks about it constantly. He puts his thoughts down on paper, then creates a model. He is already convinced that whatever he is promoting will succeed, long before he brings anyone else in on it.

Even this one piece of the success blueprint will work wonders for you. It's what brought me from the darkest points in my life to my greatest moments of triumph. If you have been doing the 28-Day Challenge, you are already feeling the powerful effects of this part of the success blueprint.

My Success Blueprint Principles

Now, while the first step in my success blueprint requires unwavering belief in yourself and your product, there are six other key principles to round it out. The combination of all seven of these principles are how I made millions in network marketing. Some may look at this list of principles, scratch their head, and wonder how that can be. Others will grasp the principles upon first glance and run with it. However you react, it would be natural for you to think that it can't be this easy.

I suggest you highlight, bookmark, or underline this page. Refer back to it as often as you need. These principles will give you a clear path to success no matter what business you own.

7 Success Blueprint Principles

1. Have a great product that you completely believe in, even if your product is yourself.
2. Use a personal touch to make sure the customer feels like they come first.
3. Offer a guarantee.
4. Provide excellent service.
5. Pay your customers for referrals.
6. Advertise a low-cost product and have an upgrade ready.
7. Keep track of your customers and offer incentives to keep them coming back.

Lessons Learned and Shared

As you build an organization or sales force, the most important thing you can do for them is to get money in their pocket during their first four days. They already have an incredible start because of their emotional high for your product. Reinforce that. My sponsor gave me leads that made me money the same day.

Whenever I had a customer who lost weight and experienced better health, I would call them and talk to them about how they could make money from their results. If they weren't interested, I would add them onto my monthly newsletter list where they could see how others, just like them, were growing and making money. Each newsletter update that I sent out, with news of increased income and health success stories, I would get ten to twenty calls from people wanting to register with me or buy products.

I'd send a copy of the newsletter to everyone within my group, then they would add a personal touch and send it to every person they had come into contact with—especially those who had shown an interest in making more money, working from home, or improving their health. To this day, my people use that newsletter and it still works. I encourage my subscribers to reach out to me if they need help, have questions, or would like the kind of checks we receive.

Over the years, I have had hundreds of people who signed up, but then had no idea what to do next. They would call and ask for my help. My policy has always been to help them, regardless if I get paid from their work or not.

The books I have read on the Law of Attraction, and the Bible, all teach the principle of giving back and helping all who are in need. If I hadn't helped Bob Anderson, he might not have helped me by encouraging me to write a fourteen-page mailer that allowed me to break all records in the company.

I read a book on advertising that taught me the importance of tracking my stats so I could see what was working and what wasn't. If you skip this step, you will lose millions. There have been many times when I saw a stat from one of my people that was lower than usual, and I would immediately call that person. Invariably, they had changed the ad, or left out "FREE SAMPLES! Money-back guarantee." Other times, when the ad was exact, I checked their voicemail greeting and it was awful.

Nowadays, I can record the voicemail for them, and each package of information that goes out has me on video, audio, or in a book, telling my story. By the time a person goes through the whole package, they're ready to call whoever sent it to them and say, "I'm in!"

This catapulted all of our incomes and took away the biggest reason why people fail to sell something: the word no.

By using this method, if a person reads all the material and watches every video, and still are not interested, they can return the package for a full refund. We made people who wanted to start their own business go through three steps of elimination, and the materials allowed us to talk to millions of people a month while we were sleeping, having fun, or working.

Now with the internet you can do this easily. You can buy lists of people that want your product and send them something that entices them to purchase.

CHAPTER 13

Where Do You Get
The Customers?

I encountered a person who was in the same business that I was in. He tried to get me to purchase a system he had developed, a system he credited for the $70,000 checks he received every month. He had only been in business for three years. I hadn't made my millions yet and was desperate for answers. Without a doubt I was impressed by his $70,000 checks, so I paid nearly $1,000 to attend one of his seminars.

In the seminar all he did was go on and on about how we should buy his training books, CDs, and DVDs. He spent about an hour teaching us how to manage a big team and how to keep motivated. I was devastated when, on the lunch break, I overheard someone say that they had known him when he was in company X ten years ago. He had been in the industry over thirty years and had taken the entire sales force from his previous company into the company we were now involved with.

I was furious! There was no way I could duplicate that! It was no wonder he wasn't able to give any of us any real advice on how to run our business. He had gotten in at the beginning of a company and was in the right place at the right time.

Upon further investigation, I found out that he was making $70,000 a month all right, but it was money made from selling his books and CDs. The money was not a result of being successful in the business we all had come to be trained on. Losing a thousand dollars was a lot for me at that time. It almost made me quit!

I went back after lunch and for the next three hours listened to his stories about how great it was to have money and go on exotic vacations. I sat there shaking my head as he put picture after picture of his new homes and cars, and he even made his wife stand up and show the diamonds she was wearing!

After another hour of him telling us we needed to have a dream and go out and bring as many people as we could to his next "training," I couldn't take it and raised my hand.

He seemed to be glad at the interruption and called on me immediately.

"I'm really new at this and I am wondering how you got your first people into your business."

He answered, "I had them buy the product."

I asked again, "How did you find those people that bought your product?"

He smiled and answered as if I were a child, "I had them come to a meeting and then sold it to them."

Now he was trying to get away from me, and even though I was embarrassed, I just couldn't shut up. "How did you get them to the meeting? Were these people you knew? Did you run an ad? What did the ad say? How did you afford to buy an ad if you were just starting out? How did you get these people to show up at your meeting?"

Obviously, I and everyone else had tried to get people to come and hear about our business. We had all tried to get people to buy our product, and anyone who has ever worked this kind of business knows how difficult it is to even ask someone to come to a meeting, let alone expect them to show up.

He didn't look very happy now, but he said, "There are many ways to do this. You just have to decide that you are going to be committed and go out and do it."

At this point I knew I was being obnoxious but couldn't stop myself. I really wanted to know. I really wanted to succeed. "*How* did you do it?"

Now he was defensive. "I worked my tail off. I talked to everyone I knew and I just kept at it."

I was willing to do that. "What did you say to them? What if you don't really know anyone, and your friends and family won't listen to you? Did you just walk up to strangers?"

Luckily, everyone in the room wanted the same answers, and they started to back me up, murmuring, "Why don't you answer her questions?

Success Doesn't Have to Be Hard

We have all seen it. A fly bumping into a window pane for hours. He will hit the same glass pane over and over again, even when there is an open window or door nearby.

That poor fly is working really hard to get out. He will hit the glass harder and harder. After a while he may rest, or worse, knock himself out, falling to the window sill. Then he'll go at it again. Sometimes he will die trying. If only he would sit back, look around, and with almost no effort, fly through the open window or door. It was always there. It was always easy. He just didn't see it. He just didn't know about it.

Most people I know who fail in their career failed for the same reason. They did not have the knowledge or were unaware of the opening that had always been there. Most of us work hard. Some of us put in 12- or 14-hour days trying to make a career or business work. We put everything we have into making a success of our venture. Unfortunately, if you are working hard on things that don't work, you will end up failing.

That's why so-called gurus often do more harm than good. They rarely give concrete help that would prevent us from hitting the glass pane. In fact, they can actually box us in and drive us to despair if we are not careful.

Attracting Customers

Think about what entices you to try or buy something. How about when you are at a Costco or your local grocery? What is something that allows you to try a new product with no chance of getting ripped off or being disappointed? It's the magic of the FREE SAMPLE.

When I got involved with my company, there was no one in the entire company of millions of salespeople using this technique in their ads. The few that had attempted it did not apply it to their business correctly. It was one of the biggest reasons I was able to break all records in a few short years, and the company had been in existence for fifteen years.

You have to do this right, though, or you can lose a lot of money. I remember being afraid to do this because each sample cost me 50 cents back then. Now, it is funny to think that I was so broke and desperate that 50 cents was a big deal to me. You have to do exactly like I did, or it can really ad up, especially if you are on a small budget. A free sample can even be intangible goods. AOL built their entire business on offering one free month of internet service if you signed up "NOW."

Lessons Learned and Shared

The beauty of the free sample strategy is that it's easy to share by word of mouth. In fact, when someone tells you about their business, tell them about your free sample or your free offer. It costs you nothing.

CHAPTER 14

Understanding Ad Basics

A lot of people think that the only reason I have been so successful is because I am a great salesperson. Nothing could be further from the truth. The cornerstone of my philosophy has always been, and will continue to be, to follow the successful people. As long as I emulate how the major billion-dollar companies do it, I will succeed. They have already spent the millions of dollars necessary to study, analyze, and test what works—and what doesn't.

People also believe that since I teach these methods, that I am somehow immune to their influence. That is also far from the truth. It's been said that the best salespeople in the world are the easiest to be sold. On two different occasions advertising basics were used on me, with my full consent, and I ended up succumbing to them just like anyone else.

Mercedes Knows How to Sell

Some great examples of this are commercials for Mercedes. They usually advertise the car that the largest number of consumers can afford to buy. They show the lowest price on TV. You will usually see an asterisk beside that price, where it says in small print, "Does not include upgrades."

When you go into the Mercedes showroom, what happens? You see the most incredible, beautiful, and expensive cars they have. The ad that lured me in was for a Mercedes car that cost around $35,000. It interested me, and I decided to check it out. Do this yourself. Go to a dealership and ask to see the car from the commercial, and see what the salesperson says next. It usually goes something like, "This car is just like it, except that it has GPS, state-of-the-art stereo system, dual heat controls, leather interior, hand stitching, and a neat new phone system."

I swear that the fancier car even smells different!

The dealership I visited had the advertised car way out back, and they forced me to walk through the showroom. Brilliant, by the way. Needless to say, all of these subtle things wore me down and I bought the most expensive car in the showroom—about $225,000 I think—with every single gadget I could get.

The Porsche Guys Must Know the Mercedes Guys

Years later, I did the same thing at Porsche. I was just going in to buy a second car. There was an ad on television that said you could be in a Porsche for $999/month. This was a far cry from my factory worker days, when I was fretting over 50-cent samples. So I convinced myself that I'd go look just for the thrill of it.

By no means was I serious about buying, but the ad drew me in to look. Steps from the dealership's front doorway, I saw a bright-yellow Turbo Carrera with stunning red seat belts and incredible cool gadgets. It was so beautiful, sexy, and fun. The Porsche Boxer they had been advertising was, once again way, in the back. It looked sad after seeing that gorgeous Carrera. I bought the Carrera that day.

I often got pulled over for speeding in Palm Beach. Every time the police officer would ask if I knew why they had pulled me over. Each time I replied, "I'm driving a bright-yellow $300,000 car." They laughed and let me off with a warning.

Three Strikes, You Are Out

Now that I think about it, the same thing happened with my Realtor. I called on a house she had posted on the internet. The house was priced around a million dollars. I told her I didn't want to see anything over a million dollars, since it would be a second home. Over the phone she didn't push me, and she didn't tell me that houses on the water in Florida were running closer to $2 million.

You can probably see that the same techniques were applied in this scenario. My Realtor showed me those million-dollar homes, and then she offered to show me one more house that was perfect for me, though a little more expensive. It's important to note that before I called this particular Realtor, I called two other real estate agents. I told them I wanted to buy a house on the water for no more than a million dollars, but they didn't know basic marketing techniques and proceeded to tell me that it was impossible. So, I went on to look for a different agent.

Those two agents lost out on a commission for a $2 million house that took less than an hour's work.

The same thing happens in network marketing. For some reason people are taught to sell a $200 product. Out of ten people, the statistics show that only two will buy. If you sell a lead-in product through FREE SAMPLES at around $30 (this amount has been tested), and give them samples of your other products that you know they need, you will get eight out of ten people that buy, upgrade, give referrals, or join you in your business.

I bought the Florida house that day for $1,895,000. No wonder that Realtor advertised herself as one of the top agents. She followed the basic rules. If she had tried to sell me over the phone, before she met me and before she established a rapport, I wouldn't have listened. I would have probably been scared off and not have met with her at all.

The Three Basics of Advertising

1. Advertise FREE items.
2. Advertise to get your foot in the door.
3. Advertise to get upgrades and referrals.

If I had known those three advertising tips when I first started, I would have grown even faster than I did. I do not guarantee this book will make you successful. However, it can help you by giving you the tools and fundamentals of marketing and advertising. It's up to you to apply them.

The best advice I have ever received was about how to decide whose advice, training, or guidance I should follow: **Look at the check of the person giving the advice and ask how long they have been in the company.**

Don't get sidetracked by anyone who cannot prove what they are telling you! Imitate what successful companies and corporations do. Why? Because they are successful and they have *already tested it*. The little guy (me, you, or any start-up) has the excitement, drive and will to succeed in their endeavor. Otherwise, they would be working for someone else and not reading this book. They usually don't have a lot of money to burn and have to get things right or they go broke.

Copy what the most successful businesses have already proven, instead of taking unnecessary risks. Look at companies such as McDonald's, Mercedes, Coca-Cola, Dell, Sprint, and Microsoft. Study their advertising and observe what has made them successful. Notice how successful companies stay with the ads that are working. Smart business people, and companies, will keep an ad in play if it is working. They might test a new ad or idea, but they never stop an ad that is working.

You will know if an ad is working if it pays for itself. An ad might not pay for itself upfront, so be smart. If the initial sale brought you back-end sales, upgrades, and referrals, it did pay for itself.

Advertising the Free Stuff

Have you noticed that every major makeup counter in any high-end store offers a free makeover? Revlon, Clinique, Estée Lauder, and Lancôme all do this. Some will have salespeople in the aisles with free samples of lotion, perfume, and aftershave they try to spray on you as you walk by! They are trying to get their foot in the door. They are trying to get you to stop and sit down. That's the main thing you want to do as a business owner. Get people's attention and get them to listen.

Now, imagine that, after the salesperson sprays you with perfume, she tries to sell you $200 worth of products. Contrast that to the salesperson who knows basic marketing and gives you a free half-hour makeover where they will pamper you, give you attention, and explain the targeted products to you. You get so excited that you just have to have them, and you don't even blink when the cashier rings up $200 because you chose those suggested targeted products, and the salesperson taught you the value of them!

What if they went one step further and told you that everyone would be asking why your skin, makeup, and hair look so good? In fact, you could earn something FREE if you told them about the saleperson that helped you.

Advertising to Get Your Foot in the Door

Advertise and open with your lowest price. Offer the product that the customer experienced immediately after you have established a relationship with them. Then listen to their needs so you can upgrade by giving them samples that fulfill their need. Successful companies advertise their most affordable, and easiest to understand, product to get you into the door.

Advertise to Upgrade and Referrals

Once a company has attracted your attention, they will do everything they can to upgrade you, sell you more, and get your address, phone number, or email address. Copy this technique!

Another technique to imitate is giving incentives to your customers for referrals. If you can get phone numbers, addresses, or emails of potential new customers, you have more opportunities. If they do not buy, add them to your mailing list and send them special offers. Send them a post card advertising a special rate, new products, or a sale. These are all top sales techniques that you should be using in any business you are in.

Lesssons Learned and Shared

Every detail adds up. If you don't utilize basic marketing strategies, you will be leaving money on the table every day.

If you have a sales force, remember that everything you do is an example for your team. They will imitate what you do. If you don't make it easy, simple, and fun, and let the materials do the work for you and your sales force, then they will burn out.

CHAPTER 15

Additonal Advertising Pointers

I remind my students, and network marketing partners, that there is no honor in suffering. Refuse to take the slow road to success. Don't get caught up in the story of the tortoise and the hare. The only thing the hare did wrong was take a nap before he crossed the finish line!

I desire to help you change, and turn everything you have ever heard about marketing, sales, and advertising upside down. They are interrelated and all are necessary when starting your own business. When done right, one flows into the other.

Refusing to use these proven techniques is the single most common reason I see people acting like the fly and wasting their time banging against a window pane when there is an open door a few feet away. They are working hard. They are putting in long hours, but they refuse to step back and see what other flies have done to make it outside or through that open door.

Insanity is doing the same thing over and over and expecting a different result.

"Insanity is doing the same thing over and over and expecting a different result." I read that somewhere and understood it immediately. When you are doing the right thing, it works. When you are doing the wrong thing, it can be disastrous.

Please Trust My Knowledge

To this day, I still have people who refuse to listen, even after show-ing them how to work smart. I have gone to extreme measures in order to provide proof of my success: pictures of me riding horses, floating in a pool, and riding my jet ski. I have accomplished a hun-dred times more, and in a tenth of the time they have invested, but decades later they are still struggling. Why? Because they refuse to learn, and they refuse to change.

Additional Ad Secret #1: Create A Sense of Urgency

Most retail stores will advertise a special sale, using words like, "One-Day Only, Labor Day, President's Day, Black Friday." Why? Because it works. It creates a sense of urgency. It makes people feel as though they have to do something important: They must "Act Now," or risk missing out. The consumer believes they might lose out or the opportunity will be given to someone else. This is a tech-nique that you just copy! It is a proven method that works.

Additional Ad Secret #2: Offer Money Back Guarantee

In this day and age, most of us will not buy anything that is not guaranteed. If you cannot guarantee your service and product, you should not be selling it. Get involved with something you love. Sell something you truly believe in.

Additional Ad Secret #3: Recognize You're Everyone

Every statistic about how "recognition" works tells us something very important. Scientists have distilled down to three primary reasons why people do the things they do. They are love, money, and recognition. What do you think is first?

If you're like me, you probably guessed that love or money was first, but we were both wrong. Recognition is the number one reason people do the things they do. Remember this, study it, and understand that people want to know that they matter. They want service. They want someone to care.

Recognition can come in the form of awards, bonuses, gifts, or a simple thank-you card. When I didn't have the cash to pay out promotions, I gave people something that would benefit their business. I gave my downline the extra leads I had generated using inexpensive posters. Incidentally, those posters advertised my FREE SAMPLES and money-back guarantee.

Recently, I saw a poster that had been placed at a main intersection. It read: "Massage. First half hour free." Brilliant!

I saw another poster that mentioned a house cleaning service that paid for referrals.

My first promotion for my newly sponsored people was simple. If they would listen to a tape on sales, attend a training seminar, and afterward could answer my questions I would give them three leads.

Then, if they could sell our $30 product to two of those leads, I would give them five more leads. I built a sales force through my retailing efforts. I would get people to buy one of my least expensive products, and then once they felt good about that product (usually only about four days), I followed up with them. Then I sold them more and upgraded them. When it was all said and done, they were already trained.

I made it so simple. All they had to do was what I did. Sell one product with a free sample, money-back guarantee for $30, and upgrade them after four days. They were also taught to get a new customer's information and let the customer know that if they supplied referrals, they would get discounts or a cash reward.

My first month in business I sent out a handwritten, cut and paste newsletter. I recognized my customers and printed their words of praise for my great product. I also recognized the three customers that had been smart enough to save money, and even make money, by giving me referrals.

I mailed it out to friends, family, and anyone else regardless if they had bought from me or not. It was less than twenty people. I doubled my sales with that newsletter and landed two more customers that wanted to give me referrals. I remember them asking me if they would be featured in my next newsletter.

Additional Ad Secret #4: Follow-Up

Statistics have shown that people need to see, or hear, something three to five times before they buy. You can do an inexpensive post card, newsletter, and automatic emails. Follow-up is also more advertising. When someone sees it over and over, they begin to notice it and even believe in it. Pepsi, Coke, Sprint, and AT&T have all been around a long time. They are well-known, so why are they still paying for commercials, billboards, and mailings? Because it works.

Additional Ad Secret #5: Testimonials

Take a good look around at advertising that you know is successful. What is a common theme that you see in almost every effective ad? They all show satisfied customers with believable testimonies.

Additional Ad Secret #6: Focused Message Is Key

Another characteristic of an effective ad is a focused message. Coke doesn't try to sell you all of their products at once. They will usually focus on only at a time, or perhaps mention one other. They know that it's easy for the consumer to get confused, overwhelmed, and unwilling to buy. A lot of businesses make the mistake of advertising so many different options that consumers end up confused and buy nothing. They walk out, hang up, or tell the eager salesperson, "I need to think about it," or, "I need to talk to my spouse." When that happens, the consumer was most likely overwhelmed with too many choices.

Lessons Learned and Shared

Pay attention to and study the commercials you see and hear. The key to any business is advertising correctly! It's not talking to friends and family

Develop your own tools. Record yourself selling your product and explaining the marketing plan. Understand that in order to get to the top fast, you have to talk to 10,000 people a day. Go to www.chriscarley.wordpress.com and listen to the audio: "How to Talk to 10,000 People a Day."

Have your voicemail recording that says, "If you are *serious* about wanting to lose weight and earn extra money working from home, you must leave your name number and email. I will send you a link on exactly *how* to feel great, lose weight, and earn extra money in your spare time." That voicemail will help weed out the people that aren't serious, and who will only waste your time.

Call people that have gotten results with your product or business and make an audio recording of at least ten people. Make a product results recording, and another about success stories of people earning extra income. Be sure to use a variety of people from all walks of life. Young people, older people, single mothers, truck drivers, and executives. This way the people hearing your recording will be able to identify with someone. On the product recording, get people that were successful in losing weight, obtained more energy, started sleeping better, etc.

We had an internet library where you could check on someone you identified with. Truck drivers, new mothers, students, lawyers, doctors, you name it, we had a testimonial for it. Those testimonies would mention other products that had changed their lives too and that made us sales while we were sleeping.

CHAPTER 16

Shoestring Advertising

I often explain to those who me ask for marketing and advertising advice that they don't have to spend a dime. They look at me like I am crazy. How I got started in marketing and advertising was 100% FREE. Even if you can't advertise for FREE, you can do it at a very low cost. New businesses do not need to go into debt to find their customer.

If you are just starting out, and have little to no money, doing these things will help you get the most bang for your buck when you do spend money on advertising.

Test, Test, Test. Then Test Again

Always test before you buy. Run a small ad before you buy a bigger ad. Most people go out and buy the biggest ad they can find. Once they find out it didn't work, they run another huge ad campaign. The problem with this is that by the time they find out the ad is not working, they have run out of money or maxed out their credit cards.

Test in a small circulation before you roll out. Remember: The ad is successful if it *pays for itself*. You will learn in the following chapters how just one ad can bring you upgrades, new clients, and reorders.

The Language Is the Key

Be sure that you have the right wording for your advertising, and use as many "hot words" as possible. I don't know how many times someone has come up to me and said, "I did exactly what you told me to do and it didn't work."

My reply to them is always the same: "What does your ad say?"

Sometimes they don't even know!

Sometimes they spiel off a seven-line ad that doesn't have any of the critical things on it that it should, and the ad cost them twice as much as a two-line ad that would have actually worked.

Free Still Makes Money

Double the results of your advertising by using the word "FREE" (hot word). When I first started what is now a million-dollar business, I was so broke I couldn't afford an ad. I handwrote my product benefits on little flyers, cards, and posters. I left it anywhere and everywhere I went. That's how I made my first $500.

Then I discovered the power of target marketing. Target marketing is when you target the buyer. Imagine two teams handing out flyers. One team goes to the mall and hands then out. The other team uses target marketing and leaves flyers at gyms, a place where people are already committed to looking good, losing weight, and feeling better. They leave their cards on cars that are parked at a Jenny Craig or Weight Watchers meetings. They mail a flyer about their sleep product to a mailing list of people that have bought information or products on sleeping better. They leave a flyer about losing baby weight inside *Parents* magazines at the hospitals. This is targeted marketing and it's powerful.

I used about eight dollars of my first profit to purchase a cheap stamp that said: "International company expanding. Pt and ft positions needed. $1,400–$4,800 per month. Call for free info book." I stamped every piece of outgoing mail on the outside of the envelope, package, or folder. I stamped extra hard on all my outgoing bills. I used it to stamp cards and hand them out to every salesperson everywhere that tried to sell me something.

Someone in real estate might concentrate on places where mortgage brokers, bank officers, or buyers live. How will they know where they live, work, or how to reach them? By looking at their advertising! Everyone in the local paper who places a "For Sale By Owner" ad would be their target. Or they might check public records for new birth announcements, newly married, sales of homes, etc. Sometimes these people will want to own a bigger house or buy their first home.

Obviously, if you have some money to invest, you can use these same principles for advertising more professionally. I have professional cards made up now, and instead of looking in the paper each week or delivering a flyer door to door, I buy mailing lists and have a company mail for me. Design your advertising around your budget, not the other way around.

Slick Ads to Mean Greater Sales

Remember, just because you are broke doesn't necessarily mean you have to worry about looking professional. A couple of months ago someone stuck a flyer on the doorknob of my house. Keep in mind that I live in a million-dollar neighborhood. The flyer was typed on a home computer and I called on it! (If you don't have a computer, don't make excuses. I used the library's computer when I first started. I also used Kinko's.)

If you think this method won't work for the upscale clients you want to reach, you are missing out. Just a couple of months ago I got another flyer on my door. It was a flyer for "peep holes." The flyer used phrases like, "being safe" and "knowing who was at the door." It mentioned their company's name, gave references, a guarantee, and a free estimate. All hot words!

I had my assistant call to get the peep hole installed. The kid came out and installed it with no problems. I told the kid that he could mention my name to my neighbors. A week later later, I noticed that three of my neighbors also had a peep hole installed. The same thing happened with lawn services, tree trimmers, pool cleaners, maid service, window cleaners, and dry cleaning businesses. I've gotten these advertisements on my door. These flyers work. My home in Florida is worth around $3 million, and you can reach people like me with little or no money. Just use the right words in your advertising. (Stay out of places where it is prohibited by law.)

Lessons Learned and Shared

No excuses! These basic marketing and advertising principles are proven to work. Think outside the box. I don't have a college degree, I never studied advertising, and I couldn't afford to go to school or buy the books, but I didn't let that stop me. Invest in yourself by taking the time to study and work on your personal growth.

Devour books that will change your thoughts, and picture in your mind the end result you want every single day. *Think and Grow Rich* by Napoleon Hill and *The Power of Intention* by Wayne Dwyer are two books you can start with.

Implementing these easy strategies will allow you to cruise through that open window easily.

CHAPTER 17

Managing the Business You Love

I used to work from midnight to seven in the morning, and then go to three-hour blueprint classes afterward. Oftentimes, I would fall asleep at work while going to the bathroom and get woken up by someone pounding on the lavatory door. Then I'd be written up. After too many write-ups, you would be fired.

My co-workers laughed at me when I asked, "Is this really all there is?" My older sister, who also worked there, along with my father, grandfather, uncles, and cousins, sat me down and said, "Yes. This is all there is. Be happy that you have a job."

I couldn't quit. I needed money for food and rent. I couldn't save enough to get ahead. I worked so much overtime, and attended so many classes, that I didn't even have time to explore other career options. It felt like a death sentence for me. I became sick working those hours. I became emotionally beaten up, and I finally told myself I'd had enough.

I had to find a way out. The library became my mentor since I couldn't afford to buy books. I read the words of Zig Zigler, Og Mandino, Wayne Dyer, Tony Robbins, and Claude Bristol. I kept searching for answers that the successful people before me had obviously found.

I knew I was better off than millions of other people, but I also felt if I could just get some guidance, then maybe I could prove that there was a better way. I wanted to be able to not only help me and my family, but the millions of people who felt the same way I did. That's why I've written this book.

Never Look Back

When I finally began to experience success, and my network marketing business took off, I made a promise to myself to help others, even if I didn't get paid to do it. I wanted to develop a plan that would continue to maintain and multiply my success for me and my downline. So I came up with a five-part maintenance program.

Part 1: Keep Your Customers Buying From You the Rest of their Lives

This seems obvious, but since 30% of all new businesses fail in the first two years, 50% during the first five years, and 66% during the first ten. What this says is that most people don't understand how to do it. Recognize your customers and clients that keep coming back, and the ones that give you referrals. Even Donald Trump does a monthly newsletter with pictures featuring members, accomplishments, and events, including enticements to attend the events, which generates more cash. I, along with all of the members, would clamor to see if our pictures would be in it that month.

Follow up with everyone on major holidays, birthdays, anniversaries. Use the same tools that the top billion-dollar companies do! When you know one of your leaders is going through a rough time in their lives, call them. When you see someone under you doing $10,000 a month in sales, call and thank them. Recognize them and interview them about how they were able to succeed at such a high level. Then put that information out to everyone.

Part 2: Always Get Referrals

Ensure that each customer is happy with you and are referring their friends, family, and acquaintances to buy from you. Give them an incentive to refer people to you. If every one of your customers, past and present, were to refer just two people to you, your business would triple.

You don't always have to pay cash for referrals. Pay them using a product that you know could make a difference in their life. Recognition can get people to compete against each other to bring you more business.

Part 3: Get Upgrades

ALWAYS get the email address of every customer who has ever bought from you or asked about your service.

ALWAYS be prepared to promote yourself and your business—whether you are at the grocery store, in line at the department store, or anywhere else. Perhaps you overhear someone complain about not being able to sleep, or that they have no energy. Any conversation that you hear where someone is talking about a problem that your business can solve, be ready to talk to that person, hand them your business card, and let them know you have a solution for their problem.

Take advantage of every up-to-date tool that is available. Treat your business like a million-dollar business and it will respond like one! I'll say it again, because it's so important:

Treat your business like it's a million-dollar business.

I know for a fact that Donald Trump only talks to people that have been cleared as being serious players and have the $300,000 to join. As a member of his West Palm Beach Golf Club, and as someone he mentored, sometimes daily for over six years, I learned a lot about business. You have to know that key players are invested.

What is better than you personally calling every single customer to let them know about your great new product or service? Letting technology do it for you! Information CDs, DVDs, newsletters, websites, direct mailing information, and informational text messaging can all be utilized to reach your target market.

How many people can you personally talk to without becoming exhausted? How many marriages are broken up because of fifteen-hour days, no vacation, and no fun time? How much of your children's lives have you missed working overtime, trying to get that raise? If I am only working four hours a day, but getting ten times the same results that you are working fourteen-hour days, seven days a week, then I am working smarter than you.

My group and I talk to more than one million leads a day. Everyone is taught to speak to at least 10 people a day. One on one. How can you make the income that those who came into this business 10 to 20 years before you when you are reaching such a small demographic? While we were sleeping, I developed my retail system when I found myself repeating the same sales pitch, or information spiel, 10 to 20 times a day. It felt like I was in the factory again! That wasn't going to work. Since I was saying the same thing over and over, why not just make a recording? The people calling in could be screened, making sure that no energy was wasted on people not serious about buying. That is working smarter.

Every time you make a sale, give that person a sample along with information on another item or service you sell. Learn basic marketing language:

"I noticed that you were looking at the anti-ager night cream. If you buy it today, you will get free samples of 'X' or ten percent off."

"I know you are here to get legal advice on your real estate, divorce, driving ticket, etc., but you also mentioned you were worried about your parents. Our office also handles senior problems, trusts, wills, estate planning…."

Part 4: Listen to Each Client

Listen to each client and find out how you can help them with something emotionally. Did they tell you that their kid has asthma or trouble learning? Did they talk about how they can't sleep at night, or that they are worried about their parent's health?

If you have a health company, then include samples and information about your products that will take care of this. Make a CD or newsletter of testimonies from people that they can identify with. Let those tools do the work for you.

Whenever someone called me excited about the results that my product or business gave them, I would say, "Hold on, Sally. Is it okay if I record this for training of my staff or for others who aren't sure they want to buy?"

Don't rehearse this, let it flow naturally. It will come across as genuine, because it will be. If you are a Realtor or car salesman, listen to the needs of your customer's loved ones. Suggest that you can help them find the right car for their child going off to college. Let them know if they refer anyone to you, you can lower the purchase price or get them a better deal.

If they know a couple of people that are looking to sell their home, give them an incentive to go out there and work for you!

Whenever someone called me and wanted my product, but didn't have the money, that was the person I hired to answers the calls that were flooding in. (I didn't have to pay them, they got to earn my product!) I made a recording of myself talking to the customers that were calling for my product, so my new hire could train themselves, while I was generating more business or sleeping.

The recording was with real people and their real questions. Later, I made a recording of satisfied customers whose testimonies helped sell the same product to other people who were interested. Real people doing the work for you! Every waiting room across the world is filled with people who have nothing to do. It could be your waiting room. Put up a television with a loop of all the services you offer. If they are coming to your spa, doctor's office, or showroom, use your satisfied client base to sell them on something else.

Part 5: Residual Income

You and your business can create an implement a residual income product that brings in cash cash in while you are asleep, on vacation, or watching your child play sports. Such a product can create an income stream that surpasses your regular income.

I am amazed that my industry is forever under fire about income testimonies. No one makes movie stars, athletes, and other successful dreamers offer disclaimers to people who are paying for training in hopes that they themselves will make it to the big time, although less than 1/10th of 1% will ever make it. For that matter, big companies on the stock exchange should have to give disclaimers that say something like, "Don't think you can achieve the same success as we did because our incomes and our company's success is not the norm."

Lessons Learned and Shared

I find that those not doing well in life and business are not sharing and helping others. So many times on social media I see a message that announces a person's success, but gives no information on how they did it. I message the person and ask them to tell us how, but they give me an excuse and refuse to share what is working for them. That person just lost hundreds of thousands of dollars, because if they would have shared, they would have been added to my elite team that shares what is working for them around the world.

Karma works in everything. What you give out comes back to you multiplied. When you help others, and operate from a mindset that believes there is enough for everyone, the right opportunities and people appear.

CHAPTER 18

Two Case Studies of Failure

When I first started in network marketing, the entire company's training consisted of talking to friends and family. This is the absolute worst thing a person new to network marketing should do! I can't believe that so many companies still push that as a viable option, when all it does is force people to have less friends and less family.

I understood right from the start that having someone call you because they had seen your ad and were informed about your product was 100% better than cold calling and begging others to buy something they knew anything about. My network marketing group was doubling and tripling because I'd taken away the rejection factor. If someone saw our ad and was not interested, they would throw it away, and it did not bother us because we didn't know!

When people called us, even if they got an inexperienced person, they knew all about our product, what it costs, and the benefits because of the information packages we sent out. Since we weren't trying to oversell on their first call, everyone calling could afford it, which made the new person excited!

This is an entirely different way to market, but it is also a better way to market. By focusing on customers that wanted my product, I could put them through the entire success blueprint without shame or guilt. Too often I see businesses failing because they don't know how to involve that eager customer in their success.

Case Study #1

My mother and I go to a nail salon near my home in Arizona. It's a beautiful establishment, but almost always empty. The new owner went out of her way to make us feel welcome. She offered us wine, gourmet coffee, and expensive bottled water. Freshly cut flowers were beautifully spread throughout every area. Yet the owner could not understand why the place was still empty.

"It's summer, it always slows down," they answered us, when we asked where all the customers were.

Both of the nail techs had kids to feed, mortgage payments, and parents they were taking care of. They were anxious about the drop in income and talking about getting night jobs. They didn't understand that they could easily double and triple their incomes by following the principles outlined in the success blueprint.

Advertise Yourself

"What are you doing to advertise yourself?' I asked both of them.

They looked at me blankly.

"You should start with the client base you have now. We've been coming to you for two years and not once have you offered us something if we referred someone to you. You should have cards that you give out to every single person you work on, offering them a free pedicure if they refer five friends.

"You should have some kind of card that lets your clients know that if they come in to see you once every two weeks for a month, that you'll give them one small extra treatment."

Know Your Customer

I told them, "Develop an information card on each of your customers that tells you what they prefer. Make detailed notes reminding you of important details about your client. Their birthday, the names of their kids, whatever they've shared with you so the person bonds with you and is more likely to always ask for you and refer their friends too."

The Real Power of Coupons

I continued, "If you know that summers are slow, offer your clients a five-dollar-off Summer Special, or first-time client special. Make your own flyers at the nearest Kinko's, and go next door to the Chinese restaurant and offer a special discount to the management if they'll let you leave a few flyers in the window. You can do the same for the twenty businesses that are located in this same strip mall. Talk to the owner of the salon about advertising to the homes that are in a ten-mile radius of you."

Know Where You Are Meeting Your Customers

"Where have most of your clients come from?" I asked.

"The restaurant next door," they both answered, but added, "We think."

"Where else?"

No answer.

"You have to know. Understand that anyone in sales who receives commissions or tips is really working for themselves. When people come in and ask for you specifically, it shows the owner how valuable you are, not to mention that you will make more money.

"I used to pay the paperboys five dollars to add my flyer to the newspapers they were rolling, and I had every family member and friend handing out flyers for me wherever they went. I even had nice bumper stickers that I put on my car and the cars of relatives that were helping me. I rode my bike and dropped flyers on front porches that were in a ten-mile radius of me. I had a three-million-dollar house on the ocean in Palm Beach, Florida, and I got a flyer on my doorstep advertising 'peep-holes.' That flyer cost him almost nothing and he told me it was his best income producer. I also got my pool cleaner that way, and when my landscaping guys didn't give me good service, I found a new lawn care company that way too.

"There are thousands of houses near here that don't know there is a beautiful nail salon right next door. You have to let them know you're here and that you offer all these opportunities for them to earn a pedicure or manicure. Be sure to mention that your salon gives out free wine, gourmet coffee, and snacks. I don't know of any other salon that does that!"

Handling the Phone

The phone rang and my nail tech had to stop my pedicure and answer. She gave the person calling the prices for the treatment they were asking about and then hung up without getting an appointment. The second call, the other girl answered and the same thing happened.

"What do you do to get the person to make an appointment?" she asked, frustrated.

"The first thing you want to do is tell the person your name," I responded. "You want to start a relationship. After you answer their questions you tell them that you are offering a special five-dollar discount if they want to book right now, and you tell them about your referral program and incentive card you will give them once they come in. Then you say, 'I have an opening today at this time, and tomorrow at this time. Which time is best for you?'

"If they still say they'll just call back, you can say, 'Great! I'm looking forward to meeting you. Our salon is rated A, and we have twenty beautiful stations, with each chair giving you a deep massage during your treatment. We've just remodeled and offer free iced coffee and drinks.'"

The Power of Follow-Up

My mom chimed in. "Cookies! When I first came here, they gave out free hot chocolate and cookies. I told all my friends about it, and they all came in and brought their friends. We drive twenty minutes even though other salons are closer." She paused. "But I felt kind of bad when they all came in and you never thanked them, or mentioned that they had come in and asked for you."

Again, they both nodded.

"Don't feel bad that you've haven't done this in the past. There are a lot of businesses out there that don't follow up. Advertising works, but follow ups keep them coming back, and bringing their friends. You should know when their birthdays are and call or send a post card to them with a special deal. If you haven't heard from a regular client for a while, mail out a 'We miss you' card with incentives and an expiration date."

Wrap-Up

My mom and I left the salon that day, hoping that they would take our advice. So many service businesses find themselves struggling unnecessarily, because they forget one thing. Service. As our economy matures, everything has become a commodity. The actual product itself can be found on every corner of every street in every town. If you cannot differentiate yourself with world-class service, what do you really have?

Case Study #2

What I did, and what you are going to do, is copy the most successful businesses you can think of. Those successful companies use the same basic blueprint to start. Why not just use the blueprint they all use? People lose money because they go off on their own instead of copying what has already been proven to work. They get excited about letting everyone know that they have the best product around and blow most of their money on advertisements that don't work. They go into debt, then quit their life's dream of owning their own business within the first three months because they are broke!

The Email

The biggest mistake I see when talking to a new person is that they think they will improve upon whatever you give them that has already worked. It's crazy.

As of this writing one of my really good golf girlfriends placed a $1,200 ad and lost all of her money. Like all the other times, of those who did this before her, she blamed me! Ignore her grammar (English is her second language) and read her exact email:

> Hi Chris,
> I know you are busy, but I need at least once help, not only by email. I do not understand Leads, how this is working and also Media Share, to buy. I have sent flyers, cards, newspaper ads, sent emails and talk and talk to people, gave samples and have sent DVDs no response. Bought 7 Kits and products for 4000.00 $ and only sold to a friend $80 and signed in one person.
> A top person and also from big check told me, I can't do it myself somebody has to show me, they all—supervisor I spoke—got it shown from their mentor.
> I know you are not interested on me, but please help as I have sold things to pay the products and I am leaving in 10 days and it is sitting under my bed until Nov. Every day I spend 4 to 5 hours on H_____ and cost of $4500.00 !!
> You did not give me one answer of my questions.

I feel so alone, please give me at least somebody to help, if you don't want to do it.!! Show in person as the other mentor do. On the iOffice, I finally got it, thanks to Naurene, but I can't find the word Task Manager to log in the Success Workbook.

I also signed in under you in the Touchfon since a month, never get any massage, only pay for it. In Anaheim I didn't see Debbie, She could find me thru the Australian girls, last night I went out with them and I met nice people the 1st day and as they saw how Lonely I was, they asked me to come with them and their Mentor. Once I understand it is easy.

This Is Why I Wrote the Book

This is the very letter that inspired me to write this book. I wrote it for everyone out there who is confused and losing money. Be sure to note that she wrote letter to me after I gave her everything I know, plus sent her to a three-day workshop that instructed her to not reinvent something that is working. Make your money first. When you have enough money that you can experiment without hurting yourself, then test out your new ideas.

The important lesson here? You have to follow what is working. The first rule is: Never change an ad that is working before you test that change.

Trust Me, I Know What I'm Talking About

I told her multiple times, and even in writing, "Do not place an ad until I check it and make sure it is right." What do you think her response? It was the same response I have received hundreds of times.

"I DID IT EXACTLY WHAT YOU SAID!"

What do you say? "Please email me the ad you placed." They will argue and say it is a waste of time. Be calm and insist that they send you their ad. Once you have received it, have them get out the materials you gave them and read what it says.

There will be a pause, and then you will probably hear, "So, I changed it a little. You think you know everything! It is still the same ad."

"No, it isn't. It may only be three words short, but it is the three words that have to be in any ad that works! Money-back guarantee?"

Couple that with two more words—"FREE SAMPLE!"—and your ad becomes all the more powerful.

Note: If you are not selling something that you believe is the greatest thing in the world, then you are in the wrong business and you need to find something that you believe in.

Use the age-old blueprints for marketing. They are there for a reason. They give you a competitive advantage over those that ignore them.

CHALLENGE 2: Do Each Essential Step

What happens if you are building a home and you don't follow the blueprint? What if you decide to leave out the foundation? These questions are basic yet some people starting their own business leave out essential steps, intentionally or unintentionally. Then they wonder why other people in the same industry are doing better than they are. These same people find themselves going into debt just to play catch up, and end up no further ahead.

If you take away only one thing from my book, let it be that **you cannot skip the basic essentials of marketing and advertising.** I have written this to reiterate how important this is.

Once, I taught a two-day seminar. About two months later I reached out to my students. Now, I know for a fact that this group of earnest and eager students understood what to do, and how to implement all the marketing and advertising strategies that I had drilled into them during the seminar. I asked questions, they answered back verbatim. I brought up points, they nodded their heads in agreement. Once the seminar was over, they all made the pledge to follow my example.

So imagine my horror when, just two months later, I talked to them and discovered that had retained next to nothing. I asked them to get on our live communication system and tell the nine to fifteen thousand people listening what they got out of the two-day training. Some of the summation I received on my training system was, "It's not what you do, it's that you do a lot of it and you talk to more people."

My mouth dropped open.

I listened to the next person. "It doesn't matter if you don't know what to say, just reach more people."

The next guy said, "I learned that whoever has the most advertising out wins."

I almost fell out of my chair. They had only understood a tenth of everything I taught! It does matter what you say. Can you imagine if you are a car salesman and walk up to people and say, "Your car looks like crap. You need to buy a new one from me." Or if your advertising said that?

You could put a million dollars into that ad and not have it attract customers as well as, "Test drive your dream car for free. Free appraisal on your current trade-in." You do have to have the essential "buzz words" in your ads.

The thing that bothered me the most about the responses from my students was that I knew people were only able to absorb about 10% of new information they receive. I also knew that everyone learns in different ways, and that I should have provided a DVD, a book, and a CD to the students.

I love the fact that technology allows us to answer someone back immediately. I realized that if those people were confused after being with me, hundreds of people that were still struggling in my downline were also confused. I knew from experience that no matter how loud I speak when I try to get something essential across, if I am speaking the wrong language, they wouldn't be able to understand me. In essence, this was the message I left:

Be very careful about just missing one step. Be especially careful about not teaching your new sales force each of the steps.

Most all of you understand how important it is to advertise your new business. You have to understand that it is important what you say. It's important how and where you advertise also.

Let's say you are selling multi-million-dollar homes, country club memberships, or luxury cars. Would you have a booth at the local flea market, or take a full-page ad out in the unemployed newsletter? Would you buy a mailing list of families that earn under $20,000 a year, or a list of people that needed help with their debt?

Would you take out a full-page ad in a Country Western magazine if you owned a store that sold heavy metal CDs?

If you are selling lawn mowers, wouldn't it make more sense to direct mail to homeowners instead of condo owners or people who live in apartment communities?

If you have a baby store, wouldn't you want to advertise in Parents *magazine instead of singles magazines?*

Or if you are in real estate, wouldn't it be smarter to mail to people whose listing was expiring or maybe couples that have just got married?

I took a deep breath and really annunciated, "Don't forget what you say does matter!"

I went on to give them my personal testimony. "When I first answered an ad that was direct mailed to me on a health/weight loss product the guy that placed the ad said to me, 'How fat are you?' I was so stunned; I just hung up on him. I know I said this before, but that guy lost millions of dollars because if he had talked to me properly on the phone, he would have signed me up.

"Listen to your training tapes. Read the books that have been out there for years that are still top sellers. They are valuable.

"And always remember to test an ad first, and in the most inexpensive way you can. Put flyers in the neighborhood first, or leave your card in places you know your best customer base is located. If your ad pays for itself, keep it going and make it bigger. If that works, expand the area and get control of it. Be dominant in that area.

"Own your own backyard. Every one of my top producers, except one, came within a thirty-mile radius of me in Auburn,

Washington. The one that didn't came from Wisconsin, and he developed a line where all five of his top earners came from within thirty miles radius of him. He received a monthly check of over $60,000 once he implemented my materials.

"Ask for discounts if you run an ad for more than one week. Follow up on every lead and get referrals, upgrades, and most importantly, go through every essential step!"

I emphasized that last sentence and then pushed the Send button, putting the message out to thousands of people. Now I am pushing my "Send button" again and am giving it to you.

Do all of the steps before you say you have failed. Only then do you know if you have a winning system on your hands or not.

For things to change, I have to change.For things to get better, I have to get better.

JIM ROHN, AUTHOR *MY PHILOSOPHY FOR SUCCESSFUL LIVING*

Lessons Learned and Shared

Leaders pay attention to details. Too often people trying to become leaders think that all of their people are on track. Later, they find out that ten levels deep there's someone who isn't getting the right message, but by then it's too late and they lose good people.

Requiring stats from your people each month will tell you when someone is off track, and you can help them immediately. If you see they have talked to ten leads and made no sales, find out what they are doing differently than everyone else who are making eight out of ten sales.

Sadly I have called and found out the upline who I had helped reach $10,000 a month wasn't following through with the person, so I worked with that individual, and that's why my check grew so fast and big. If you want explosive growth, you go beneath people and work with those needing you.

I also found that sometimes my great leaders didn't hear me correctly even though I'd told them the same things over and over. I had to create a manual with exact steps and master copies of ads that worked. Whatever business you are in, you have to have audio, video, and written training because every one learns differently. Create tools in this manner that work for you so you aren't repeating yourself, and to ensure your message doesn't get watered down. Reinforce the things that are working by interviewing people who are growing.

As you start to earn a check, reinvest in your downline that are listening and following through. Don't offer promotions of vacations or dinners—give promotions that are going to cause that person to grow instantly. Advertising that works.

CHAPTER 19

My Learning Curve

My mind still boggles at everything that transpired once I finally learned the simple rules of marketing. The same set of rules that thousands of successful people and companies had been using for hundreds of years. I made it. I became successful and made millions in just a few years. I had done well, in spite of my friends and family telling me that I was a dreamer, despite their predictions that I would go into debt. Even though they said that starting my own business and working from home was impossible.

Don't get me wrong, I was scared when I finally made the decision to try another business. Like many people, I had tried different avenues, been taken advantage of, promised success if I invested my money. I lost not only my money, but my confidence.

There were mansions and large homes in every single city in the world, and some of those were people's second and third homes. I was angry with myself because I couldn't figure out what so many other people were doing to be successful. What was wrong with me that I couldn't even earn enough for one home? That feeling made me ashamed and frustrated.

It also became my motivation.

Share the Gospel of Abundance

Traveling to more than seventy countries, and teaching these principles, I have helped tens of thousands of people. Men and women from every conceivable background. Each person with their own special set of circumstances. All of them with one goal in mind, to build a business within a business that earns a residual income.

I have known brilliant doctors with strong practices who weren't able to take off an afternoon to attend their child's big game or important event. These same people are now applying the marketing principles in this book, not to just make more money, but to make more time. While they are enjoying their families and attending these important functions, their income doesn't stop. This is significant no matter who you are. Real abundance is the ability to regain your time.

The approach that's been outlined in this book has always worked and will continue to work. The ideas and principles are not a fad or scam. Once you learn them, you can implement them into every area of your life. I used them to help a single mother of three who was living out of her car, with no phone, earn $2,000 in eight days. She handed out handwritten fliers, just like I did, using the phone booth near the car she was living in. **It's not circumstances that hold you back; it's how you define yourself by those circumstances that makes all the difference.**

Take Away Your Excuses

Evolution isn't an easy road in the beginning. A myriad of excuses get in the way of making the transition from the old you to the new you. I hope that I can help you destroy every excuse you have ever had.

Let me list a few of the excuses I have heard, or used myself:

- "I don't have enough time to do what you did."
- "It won't work for me because I have to work full-time, as well as take care of my children and my parents, and don't have a dime to invest."
- "I have to work full-time, go to school, and make time for my wife, husband, girlfriend, kids."
- "My children take all my time. I can't sacrifice what they need."

- "I don't know anyone who would buy from me."
- "I have no family, no spouse or friends to support me in my dreams."
- "I'm dyslexic and am not smart enough to keep books and records."
- "I don't own a car."
- "I don't feel good and I can't get out of bed."
- "I'm blind, deaf, have only one limb." (You probably won't hear these excuses because the people I helped who had any of these issues never made excuses!)
- "That may have worked back then, but things are different right now." (This is my favorite!)

All the above excuses are actual reasons I have heard and continue to hear today. Some of them I have used myself.

Lessons Learned and Shared

It is so easy to let the latest popular "trainer" with bright new tools they want to sell you shift you from what is working. Unfortunately, as I demonstrated through my own experiences, many of these trainers don't give you the full picture on how they truly achieved their success. So when you make an attempt to use their shiny new tool, you feel like you are the one to blame, never once looking to see that the tool itself was flawed.

After helping build thousands of people who were desperate and broke after following the wrong plan for years, I was stunned when they reached the top and decided they would rewrite the materials that got them there. I would stand by, helpless, as I watched groups consisting of thousands of successful people stop using what was working and switch to something untested. In those instances I have never been more frustrated and sad. That is why I encourage people to **stay the course**. If you have something new, test it alongside what worked before. Don't abandon one for the other, because it rarely turns out in your favor.

CHAPTER 20

Knowledge Is Powerful

Within a few years of going to the "Temple" (library) that stored the "Answers" (marketing success after success), I went from being a $10.50 an hour, out-of-work airplane factory worker to earning over a million dollars. I remember all too well how desperate and physically ill I felt while working in that factory. Working from midnight to seven in the morning, I cried every night on my way to work.

At the time I didn't know what the Universe had in store for me, and I kept visualizing the future I wanted and didn't give up. I read my motivational books even though I was ridiculed. I stood up for myself when no one else would. I persevered when everyone and everything seemed to be against me. All of this was possible because I implemented marketing materials that did all the work for me and my team.

Today, I have a lifestyle that has allowed me to hang out with Donald Trump and get to know him as a friend. I have met people like Barbara Walters, Katie Couric, former President Bill Clinton, and former President Gerald Ford, along with many more. Movie stars have filmed or been photographed in my Malibu home: George Clooney, Cameron Diaz, Lucy Liu, Drew Barrymore, and Bruce Willis, to name a few.

Who Are You Trusting with Your Dreams and Future?

Whenever I get a call or message from someone who just lost their life savings or their kid's college fund, lamenting, "I did what my mentor told me to do and it didn't work!," it makes me sick. Please don't let this happen to you.

Who are you listening to? Remember, whenever anyone wants to give you advice, ask to see their check.

When dealing with anyone trying to get you into a business deal, franchise, or sell you an ad, always ask to see their results. It's not a perfect method, but it's a method that quickly weeds out the pretenders who want to make a fast buck off of you. No system is perfect, and with my current success I have not been immune. Even with my due diligence efforts and expanded circle of influence, I still find that it's difficult to determine what the truth really is.

What Is Guru Advice Really Worth?

Whether it's sales advice, money managers, stockbrokers, network marketing gurus, or so-called investment seminar experts, advice and training are everywhere. There is so much noise, now more than ever, that it's difficult to know who to trust.

After working so hard to earn it, I watched my million-dollar portfolio in the stock market dive on CNN, in real time. I know marketing. I know advertising. I know sales. So as I moved up in the world, I made the assumption that the financial analysts also knew about their industry. I was more furious with the analysts giving current advice on what to do than I was about the market. They were the ones I followed in the first place!

Why didn't they show me their portfolios? Why didn't they tell me how much they were up or down for the year?

Then I was furious with myself. I didn't follow my own advice, and I had lost hundreds of thousands of dollars.

Why did I not demand to see how much money they had made before I followed their advice? Why would I listen to anyone or follow their plan without asking to see their track record? How many times was I going to invest my time, money, and energy without first asking to see what it had done for them? Why was I listening to anyone if they weren't successful?

When it came to network marketing, I had only gone to the most successful to learn from.

Why wasn't I doing the same thing in my other endeavors? Would I have made the same decision—spent my time learning and listening to them, have my future and family's future on the line—if I had found out that my teacher or advisor hadn't had success in that field?

I had just assumed since they were on television, or had a book published, or were teaching a seminar, they had achieved success in that field. I found out that a lot of real estate "how-to" seminar teachers, as well as some marketing seminar professionals, hadn't made any money or had actually lost money in the last ten years in that field. I found out that the only real money or success they had achieved was selling their books, CDs, and DVDs to people like me.

This was a frustrating lesson to learn, and it applies to all areas of life. You cannot take advice about network marketing from someone who has never been successful in a network marketing business, nor can you trust anyone who simply markets and promotes how to be a great network marketer without finding out exactly how they did it.

Insist on knowing the truth.

The Relationship Expert

When you are first getting into a business, career, or even a relationship, you may seek guidance. Be sure to check out whoever it is you are following. What are their results?

I was confronted with the unreliable guru phenomena once again when I bought a relationship teacher's books and tapes from an infomercial. Years later I found myself with her, backstage in the green room. For those not familiar, a green room is a TV show's waiting room for the guests to sit in until they are called onstage.

I tried to make small talk with her, but for whatever reason she was not receptive to me. So I resigned myself to just listen to her talk to one of the other guests. I overheard her talking about her first marriage. Then she was talking about her second husband. She then mentioned what her third husband was like. She had been married a total of five times!

No wonder my marriage was falling apart. I was studying the wrong plan, and obviously so was she!

Lessons Learned and Shared

I bring up these examples to show you that I'm not perfect—**no one is infallible.** I have been misled by well-meaning, and not-so-well-meaning, people throughout my life. But never once did I stop looking for the answer I wanted and knew I deserved.

I don't consider myself a guru and want to move as far away as I can from cultivating that type of image. No matter what, I am still that hardworking factory girl who took an opportunity by the horns. That helps me understand where you are. It gives me the ability to help you pull yourself up, and at the end of the day I have checks to prove it.

My advice throughout these chapters is meant to do one thing and one thing only—empower you to be who you are meant to be. You don't need a guru for that, you need a friend. Hopefully, that friend can be me.

CHAPTER 21

When Will I Be Successful?

I turned my life around and became a millionaire in just three years. If someone had told me that they had a plan that would show me how to be a millionaire in 36 months, I would have laughed at them. Yet it happened.

Without a doubt there was a confluence of events in my life at that time. I cannot promise you that you will be a millionaire or give you any type of guarantee on how much you will possibly make following my system. What I can do is ask you this question:

What does the alternative look like if you don't try?

I knew my alternative was to remain depressed, defeated, and hopeful I could find another menial and miserable job. I decided I didn't want that, so I evolved. This book is your chance to do the same.

How Long until Things Change?

When I started out, I learned very quickly that when a person is trying to sell you on following them, find out how long it took for them to get their success and what they did before that endeavor.

My first few months of trying to get my sales off the ground, I was listening to a couple who were teaching that their sales went to over $100,000 a month in only the second month in the business.

For three grueling weeks, I did exactly what they told me to do. But it wasn't working. In fact, I was going backward and was burning out.

I started to ask them questions. It wasn't easy to get near them either. They avoided Q&As and any individual questions. I finally trapped the wife in the bathroom! I found out that they had come from another sales company and brought over all their sales reps with them. I found out that they had been in this business over ten years but didn't count the first nine years because their first month of "really working" had just started. I also found out that the company I was involved with had let them teach this to thousands of other new people before me.

I actually went home and cried. I wanted to quit.

The same thing happened again when I listened to another couple give their income testimony. They kept repeating, "All we did was talk to people." What they failed to mention was that they were entering new countries illegally, and that no one else had access to these countries. They also failed to mention that they had uprooted themselves and lived in Mexico City for years.

Here I was trying to copy them, and they weren't telling me what they were really doing.

Specialized Training, Not So Special

There was one time when I paid for specialized training and flew all the way to Hawaii to learn the secrets of a successful networker from Japan. I sat in the front row, and after four hours of hearing nothing on how to improve my business, I finally just stood up and asked, "You've been telling us for an hour now that you had so many new clients and customers that your business started booming. How did you get those customers?"

He was evasive, and it was obvious he didn't want to tell me. I refused to sit down. In front of about two hundred top people I rephrased my questions. "You said that three nights a week you packed a room full of new customers. How, exactly, did you pack the room?" He started to sweat.

He answered, "It's easy to get customers, but that's not what I am teaching."

He started showing us pictures of his great office, his Rolls Royce, and his checks. I stood again. "In your area, you are not allowed to run any advertising. How did you pack a room? How can I learn to pack a room?"

What I really wanted to say was, "You have no right to get up onstage and teach if you aren't going to teach us how to duplicate you." The fact was, he didn't want to teach me. I would be his competition someday, and he didn't want to help me.

After he was off the stage, I didn't stop. By that time, I had taught a lot onstage myself and had helped hundreds of people improve their sales. One of his direct associates who worked with him came up to me. He was one of the people I trained when I had gone to Japan. At that time I taught them everything I knew. I had given them exact ads and newsletters, and shared with them our sales tools for them to copy.

He may have felt guilty that his upline wouldn't share and give back because he decided to tell me the speaker's secret. It was a brilliant marketing strategy.

Japan was a very hot market and due to the speaker running illegal ads making unrealistic income testimonies, the government would no longer let any advertising into any newspapers. The top Japanese salespeople were really hurting because of this. Yet he had found a loophole. He ran ads in all the major newspapers that said, "Free English accent lessons."

He didn't speak Japanese, but his wife did. In teaching them English slang and pronunciation, he told them about his product and business opportunity. I was so naïve when I first started, and you can learn from my naivety and not repeat my mistakes.

Lessons Learned and Shared

Red herrings and missing recipe ingredients are notorious in the sales industry. A lot of speakers have huge egos and are up there to only promote themselves. You can still learn from them, though. Keep asking questions.

The only thing that saved me was concentrating on the fact that with all this deceit, this guy from Japan was making over $2 million a year. I thought, *Let's see what I can do without using any deceit.* This was an important lesson, and one I was to keep repeating. When something negative happens to you, learn from it.

CHAPTER 22

The Wrong Plan

"You were so real! You talked from your heart and you said it like it is. Half the words you said weren't even correct and sometimes I didn't even understand you, but I could hardly put my notebook down, and I have never had such exact instructions given to me!

"Just the training you gave us on 'Free Samples' propelled my business further than anything else I had ever learned from any book or seminar that I have paid thousands of dollars for."

More than one successful CEO had waited in line just to come up and shake my hand and tell me, "After watching the first five minutes of your DVD training, I told my wife, 'She is awful, she is all over the place, and I can't even follow what she is saying,'

"Then, with my wife eyeing me, I couldn't stop myself from sitting down, closer to the TV. What you were saying really caught my attention and I couldn't stop listening. I kept asking my wife, 'How much is she earning a month?' When for the third time she told me, 'Over $10,000 a month' I grabbed some paper and started making notes!

"You had already showed me how to place an ad that really worked. That one tip could have stopped my last venture from draining our life savings! As I watched you talking from your heart, I started to laugh and nod my head in agreement, finally really getting it, and I just knew that I was going to get rich!"

What I Have to Share

I know he was really thinking that if this undereducated farm girl could make that much money, then he would make even more. After all, he had a college degree and years of experience.

Great! That is exactly what should happen. This particular gentleman reached his goal in just three years. The very first time I met him, he came right up to me and said, "If you think you can ever get me making more money than I do now and quit my job of over twenty years with Boeing Aerospace, you really are crazy. I'm going to help my wife part-time, but I don't believe you even make this much."

Who could blame him? I was still in my thirties, and even though I held a copied check of over $20,000 for that month and also had the previous checks from EACH month for the last several months laid out before me, showing each check increasing every single month, I still had trouble believing it!

I wonder what would have happened to both of us if we were to know then that my check would keep growing every single month for the next several years to way past $100,000 a month!

The Wrong 30-Year Plan

As I got to know him better, I understood why he was so afraid that I would help him reach his goals. It was the same reason why so many of us don't bother to look into something like this. If what I was saying was true, that meant that he, now in his fifties at that time, had been following the wrong plan for over thirty years! No one wants to admit that.

This is the really sad part for many of us. How can we let go of the idea that we've spent hundreds of thousands of dollars on a degree and 30 years of our lives in a job that we really didn't like? How can we let go of a job that we have invested five if not seven days a week into (not including all of the special training, continuing education classes, travel, and time away from our family)?

In addition to all of that, my friend had been spending two hours every morning and two hours every evening driving to work. How could he possibly admit that all those years following that plan had been wasted? He didn't have to and neither do you!

Every minute of every year we can take with us. In the first week of implementing the things I taught him, he tested them and experienced results right away. He was able to draw upon all those years of experience, and soon he and his wife were breaking income records just like me.

What Made the Difference?

My friend later went on to India and Dubai to lead one of the strongest financial teams in the Seattle area. So what made the difference? He followed some basic tenets when he decided to step out of his comfort zone:

1. At least try.
2. Understand that if thousands of people were making it work (especially a fired ex-Boeing worker), then he could too.
3. Realize there is nothing wrong with changing your blueprint if a new plan does the work faster and easier.
4. He decided that the only waste would be staying in the old plan even longer!

At that time, according to the national mortality stats of a man's life after he went to full retirement, at age 65, was just two years. Horrific.

My grandpa worked for that same company, and he retired at age 60. Although he didn't die at 62, he became very ill. All of the fishing trips he promised to take me on when he retired never happened because he didn't feel well enough to go.

Just Copy It!

What about your plans? Are you waiting to get married, have kids, or until you get enough money or get that promotion? That is the wrong plan!

Learn how to reach all of your goals while you are on that vacation, building that new home, riding in that new car. Instead of, "Just Do It," you need to **Just Copy It**! You have already been doing it, you just need to know *how* to do it. Follow through with the marketing plan secrets detailed in this book. Secrets that are in plain sight.

Copy me, who copied the big guys, and you will see similar, if not the same, results!

Lessons Learned and Shared

Remember, I got results with as little as $8 for my first handwritten posters. My purpose for writing this book is to teach you how to succeed right from the start. I have one goal in mind for you, and that is to put money in your pocket right away, without going into debt.

CHAPTER 23

Success at Work

When I first started reading books and learning how to succeed in my life, I was so disappointed to discover that there are a lot of books out there whose sole purpose is to make the reader excited enough to get them to buy even more books, or some training program. So many times I would spend valuable time and money only to find out there wasn't any meat or substance that I could actually use.

I have paid for massive amounts of training I couldn't afford that promised to help me make millions, and it was all a lie. I have witnessed multiple speakers get onstage and tell stories about the hardships they endured, and watched as they paraded pictures of their fancy cars, boats, and mansions. In the end, they would teach absolutely nothing that would help me to achieve the same results.

In fact, during one three-day training I attended, I literally slept in a bathtub because I was sharing a hotel room with four other women who were just as broke and confused as I was. Finally, I had enough. That's when I decided to rely on marketing basics to help me.

Success through Copying

Anytime I brought someone new into the business, I would make it as easy as possible for them. I would start by saying, "Do you love this product and want to market it? Great, you are already trained and you can start right now. Remember how I gave you a free sample and some information? Then, after a couple of days you called and placed an order? That's all you have to do now to get going. It's really that easy!"

People would be skeptical and look at me as if I had two heads. They couldn't believe it was that simple, but it was that simple then, and it is that simple today.

The Right Marketing Works for Any Business

I remember the time I met a young lady who worked at a spa I liked to visit. She knew my story and asked me for tips on how to promote her business and increase her sales on eyelash products. I get questions like this all the time. Many people simply don't follow through. So I half expected the same when I went to get a facial from her the next time I went in.

Of course the first thing I noticed was the technician's lovely eye lashes. They were incredibly long and thicker than the last time I saw her. I wanted to ask her right then what she had been doing, but waited to see if she had remembered all the marketing ideas I had given her on my last visit. I had to laugh when she allowed me get into my robe. The robe was folded nicely, and on top of it was a small card that read, "Longer lashes in 2 weeks, guaranteed!"

The product was retailing for $150, which seems like ridiculous amount, but she had listened to my advice. She told me, "I'm offering all my best clients a thirty percent discount if they buy today. I also have referral cards for you to hand out."

The wholesale price was around $60, but none of the other technicians at the spa were doing the things I had taught her. She not only outsold all ten of her co-workers, but her commissions for one week were more than triple of those who had sold without the 30% discount!

The next time I saw her, I gave her a little button she could pin on to her coat. It had two closed eyes with beautiful lashes. Under the lashes it said, "Ask me about my long eyelashes."

She forgot one thing I had taught her—she was leaving a lot of money in commissions as a result. I had stressed to her how important it was to have real testimonies, and especially before and after pictures.

Right that moment she whipped out a camera and took a picture of my "before" lashes. When she was done with my new lashes, she took another photo. I dropped by two weeks later and she had the pictures up on her wall.

No matter how good a company's literature is, everyone wants to see real people and hear authentic testimonies. We are all tired of seeing models in unrealistic advertisements. If you were to ask ten people to look at your homemade before and after pictures, then compare them to the company's slick promotional brochures, they will tell you they bought the product because of the homemade advertisement.

I was tremendously proud that she had asked for advice and then applied it. If the owner of the spa trained all of the staff in the same way, not only would they make more money, but the customers would be even happier.

Right Business, Wrong Card

I have received thousands of business cards over the years, and seldom has anyone given me a business card that brings value to me, the potential customer. Something so simple, yet 95% of people are losing thousands of dollars in commission, company growth, referrals, and upgrades, all because of an unnecessary mistake. In fact, the majority of business cards will be thrown away because of these mistakes. I am going to give you a few insights so that the next time you have business cards printed, you won't miss out on opportunities to make a bunch of money.

From Business Card to Sales Card

Obviously, you will have your name, address, phone, email address, website, fax, and a brief description of what your business is. For example:

Suzy Jones
Realtor

Business cards should be called "sales cards." Not only should the card give information about your business; they should also be made in such a way that anyone finding it would want to keep it in case they would someday use you or refer you to a friend. This is a card that gives added value to the customer.

How do you do this?

I will try and hit as many different business examples as possible. Obviously some will only apply to a certain business, but I am sure you are smart enough to match it up and come up with ideas for your own business.

Your card should

1. Make the recipient an offer.

- Free test drive when presenting this card
- Free Samples with this card
- Free drinks when you purchase a meal
- 10% off all computer packages with this card
- Free market analysis of your home's worth
- Free landscaping consultation
- Free 1/2-hour consultation of legal services

Typically, someone you hand a business card to will often have two or three cards from our competitors. How do you make them want to call you instead of someone else?

2. Give an incentive to buy from you (and not your competitor).

"We pay you for referrals." (Check what is legal for your industry, but remember, this doesn't have to always be cash.)

I once got rewarded a round of golf at a very prestigious course that would have cost me at least $400 for referring a couple of people to my Realtor, who subsequently bought a home from him.

My favorite restaurant owner, to whom I sent numerous groups of high-paying customers, will not let me pay for a meal whenever I come in. When I didn't come in for a while, because I didn't want to take advantage, they called me and sent over hundreds of dollars' worth of takeout.

My masseuse gave me free massage and a very expensive package of lotions after I had sent her two customers who hired her for weekly massages.

My dive shop nearby is so incredible. Whenever I refer groups to them, they ask me to go along when there is room, and will not let me pay.

The mortgage broker, who I have sent many people to, sent over a case of expensive wine.

Just about anyone whose services you use can be bartered with in this way when you agree to recommend them to others. For example: landscapers, attorneys, hair dressers, nail techs, accountants, and many more.

Other incentives that can be offered:

- X% discount with contract for service.
- Free rental for service checkups when you buy a Mercedes.
- Free acupuncture service when you join our Wellness Center.

3. Give them a reason to not throw away your card, and even want to ask you for more to hand out for you.

- Bring three new clients to our studio and get one month of free personal training.
- Two for one dinner entrees. Send five of your friends with this card and get your dinner paid for.

Aston Martin Dealership Secrets (You Might be Seeing a Pattern)

As you have probably figured out from reading this book, I like cars. Some of these ideas were points that came from a great salesman at an Aston Martin dealership I visited.

The first salesman I met had a plain card and hadn't bothered to use his business card as a sales card. I walked out not buying and really not being interested in buying. Nevertheless, something kept nagging at me and I really wanted to learn more about that car.

When I went back to look at it again, another salesperson gave me his card. On the card were a bunch of reasons why to buy the car from him. He offered a free rental car when my car was being serviced. He also offered a pickup service. So I bought the $175,000 DB7 from him and threw the other guy's card away.

I was kind enough to tell the first salesman that he should change his business card to a sales card, and the next time I saw him, he had done just that!

You want to make your cards an incentivized advertisement. That way, if someone found it on the ground, they would want to keep it for the day when they will want or need your product.

I have seen many business cards that left me wondering what the person was selling. Have your cards made as if they were a small ad in a popular newspaper, magazine, or billboard.

CHALLENGE 3: Be the 1 in 40,000!

Take Jim Rohn's challenge.
Write this down:

> **For things to change, I have to change. For things to get better, I have to get better. My spouse doesn't need to change, nor my family, job or my circumstance. For things to change for me, I have to change.**

Put your goals somewhere you can see them and read them out loud three times a day for 120 days, consecutively. Your first step in reaching success is to know what you want. The second step is to remind your subconscious everyday what it is. Do not worry about the how. Write down what you want first, and the how will come to you.

Lessons Learned and Shared

Success doesn't come cheaply. Few people are born with an innate set of tools that will make them successful. Success is a habit that needs to be cultivated. It begins with several small victories, a few setbacks, and then more victories, and so on. It's the setbacks that stall too many people. They use the setbacks as an excuse to give up, quit, and stop innovating. Let success be a habit for you. Let every small victory be a reason for celebration, and the big victories will follow.

Conclusion

Focus. On. The. Ones. That. Deserve. It.
MARK HUGHES

"Gramps, I can catch anything that comes to me and I am a good hitter, but compared to all the older kids, my legs are too short and I can't run the bases as fast as them," I told Grandpa, frustration in my voice.

When Gramps got excited or he had something important to say, he would grin, lick his lips, and start stuttering sounding like an engine that wouldn't kick over.

"Thaaaaa...thaaaaat...that's eeeeasy to fix!"

He talked slow, making sure I was paying attention. Then he grabbed my two hands and pulled me close, preparing to tell me a secret I'd be able to use the rest of my life.

"If you hit the ball over the fence, you can walk the bases."

Why I Wrote This Book

I have had my successes, but I promised God a long time ago that I would give back and help others. This is me giving back.

This simple book is written for the thousands of individuals I see and meet throughout my life who are living paycheck to paycheck.

It's for the people whose retirement is sufficient, and for those whose retirement is insufficient.

It's for the ones who toil away in jobs they dislike, and for the individuals who are desperate to learn how to get ahead.

It's for those who are praying for a way to change their future. I meet people waiting tables at restaurants where an expensive meal and bottle of wine cost more than they bring home in a month.

I see their questioning looks as they park my car that costs more than their home.

This book is written for old and current friends who are barely making more than minimum wage.

It's for dozens of family members working long hours to keep their families fed.

It's for the employees who work for me: the young pool cleaner, the hardworking gardener, the elderly man who washes and takes care of my boat and the bevy of yachts in front of my house, the breathless, overworked valets who run in 100-degree heat parking hundred-thousand-dollar cars at Donald Trump's private golf club, and the stewardess in private planes who stoically take abuse from spoiled owners.

And it's for the hundreds of worn-out unemployed workers waiting in line and work-weary individuals who are just slightly missing riches because they don't know the basic rules of getting ahead in life.

I notice them all, because I was one of them for most of my life.

Your Journey Is Just Beginning

All you need to do is begin. Follow the exercises, follow the examples, and then reach out to me and let me know how well they have worked for you. Send me an email on my website, www.chriscarley. wordpress.com, like me on Facebook, Tweet me, etc. Join my community and contribute to our entrepreneurial dialogue. Or you can do it the old-fashioned way and send me a letter telling me how you have used my experiences to change your life.